FTCE Educationa Specialist PK-12 Study Guide

-  **Crafting an Effective Study Plan:** Uncover the secrets to developing a customized study strategy tailored to your needs, optimizing productivity while minimizing time wastage.
-  **Unlocking Cognitive Potential:** Discover proven methods for enhancing memory retention, boosting comprehension levels, and cementing information in your long-term memory.
-  **Balancing Act:** Utilize effective time management techniques to strike a harmonious balance between your study commitments and other obligations, fostering a healthy work-life-study equilibrium.
-  **Stress Management Solutions:** Conquer exam-related stress through mindfulness practices, relaxation techniques, and resilience-building exercises, ensuring a calm and focused mindset during crucial moments.
-  **The Power of Practice:** Delve into the significance of practice exams, sample questions, and simulated tests, and uncover strategies for analyzing performance to pinpoint areas ripe for improvement.

Disclaimer of Liability:

This book aims to offer readers background information on various topics discussed within its pages. It is sold with the understanding that neither the author nor the publisher provides professional advice, including but not limited to legal or medical matters. Should professional assistance be required, readers are advised to consult qualified professionals.

While extensive efforts have been made to ensure accuracy, typographical errors or inaccuracies may exist. The author and publisher disclaim any responsibility or liability for any loss or damage, direct or indirect, resulting from the information presented herein. This disclaimer extends to any potential loss or harm caused by the information contained in this book.

The information is provided "as is," without warranties regarding completeness, accuracy, usefulness, or timeliness. Readers are urged to seek the opinion of certified experts or professionals for the most up-to-date knowledge.

This book does not reflect the viewpoints or policies of any specific organization or professional body. Any perceived slights towards individuals or groups were unintentional, despite the possibility of their occurrence.

TABLE OF CONTENT

STUDY GUIDE

Chapter 1: Introduction to FTCE Educational Media Specialist Exam

Understanding the Purpose of the Exam
Overview of the Test Structure
Importance of the Educational Media Specialist Role

Chapter 2: Foundations of Educational Media

History and Evolution of Educational Media
Theories of Learning and Instructional Design
Digital Literacy and Information Literacy

Chapter 3: Media Technologies and Resources

Print Media: Books, Magazines, and Newspapers
Digital Media: Websites, Blogs, and Social Media
Audiovisual Media: Videos, Podcasts, and Interactive Presentations

Chapter 4: Collection Development and Management

Selection Criteria for Educational Media
Acquisitions and Budgeting
Cataloging and Classification Systems

Chapter 5: Instructional Design and Delivery

Understanding Instructional Design Models
Integrating Educational Media into Curriculum
Strategies for Effective Media Integration

Chapter 6: Media Literacy and Ethics

Teaching Media Literacy Skills
Evaluating Media for Bias and Accuracy
Copyright and Fair Use Guidelines

Chapter 7: Collaboration and Professional Development

Working with Teachers and Administrators
Professional Learning Communities
Continuing Education and Professional Growth

Chapter 8: Assessment and Evaluation

Assessing Student Learning with Media
Evaluating the Effectiveness of Media Programs
Using Data for Continuous Improvement

FTCE Educational Media Specialist Exam Overview, Chapter 1

For those aspiring to become certified educational media specialists in the state of Florida, the Florida Teacher Certification Examinations (FTCE) Educational Media Specialist PK–12 exam is an essential evaluation. This thorough assessment assesses the knowledge, abilities, and proficiencies required to succeed in the position of instructional media specialist for all grade levels, starting with pre-kindergarten and ending with grade 12. This chapter will explore the objectives of the FTCE Educational Media expert exam, give a synopsis of its format, and emphasize the importance of the position of the educational media expert in the current educational environment.

1.1 Comprehending the Exam's Objective

Verifying that applicants have the necessary skills and knowledge to efficiently assist teaching and learning through the integration of educational media resources and technologies is the main goal of the FTCE Educational Media Specialist test. Educational media experts are essential in providing students with access to a wide range of instructional materials, developing their media literacy, and working in tandem with teachers to improve the quality of education in general.

The exam seeks to maintain the highest levels of quality in the industry and advance the professional growth of educational media professionals by evaluating candidates' expertise in a variety of fields relevant to educational media. For educators hoping to fill this vital position, the FTCE Educational Media Specialist exam sets a standard by rigorously evaluating teaching methodologies, subject matter competence, and ethical issues.

1.2 Synopsis of the Examination Framework

The purpose of the FTCE Educational Media Specialist exam is to evaluate applicants' knowledge and abilities in a variety of areas related to the field of educational media. In addition to multiple-choice questions, the exam includes a performance-based assessment section that gauges applicants' aptitude for using what they have learned in real-world situations.

The following subareas of the test, each concentrating on a certain facet of educational media, make up the test:

Foundations of Educational Media: This subarea assesses candidates' comprehension of the theoretical, philosophical, and historical underpinnings of educational media in addition to their familiarity with the major ideas and ideas that have shaped the field.

Media Technologies and Resources: Print, digital, and audiovisual media are among the media technologies and educational resources with which candidates are evaluated for their knowledge. Topics including media production, information literacy, and digital literacy are also included in this subarea.

Collection Development and Management: Candidates are assessed in this subarea based on their capacity to choose, obtain, arrange, and oversee collections of instructional media that are in line with curriculum requirements and instructional goals. Collection development policies, cataloging systems, and budgetary considerations are a few possible topics of discussion.

Instructional Design and Delivery: Candidates are assessed on their understanding of curriculum planning strategies for incorporating educational media, effective methods for delivering instruction utilizing media resources, and instructional design models.

Media Literacy and Ethics: Candidates' comprehension of media literacy principles, their capacity for critical thought, and the moral implications of using instructional media are the main topics of this subarea. Media analysis, copyright law, and responsible media consumption are a few possible topics.

Collaboration and Professional Development: The ability of candidates to work cooperatively with educators, administrators, and other stakeholders to support the efficient use of instructional media in classroom settings is evaluated. Professional learning communities, leadership abilities, and professional development opportunities are among the other subjects covered in this subarea.

Assessment and Evaluation: This subarea looks at how well applicants can measure the learning outcomes of their students, assess the value of media programs, and use assessment information to guide decisions about instruction and enhance procedures.

Innovation and Technology Integration: Applicants are assessed on their knowledge of cutting-edge methods for integrating technology into the classroom, as well as upcoming developments influencing the educational media industry.

1.3 Importance of the Position of Educational Media Specialist

In today's educational environment, an educational media specialist plays a multifarious and vital role. Specialists in educational media act as sparks for creativity, assisting educators in making the most of a wide range of media tools to improve teaching and involve students in worthwhile learning activities.

The skills of educational media specialists in instructional design, technological integration, and media selection enable teachers to provide inclusive, dynamic learning environments that meet the varied requirements of their students. Through the development of critical thinking abilities, media literacy, and responsible digital citizenship, they provide students with the means to succeed in a world that is becoming more and more mediated.

Additionally, educational media professionals are essential in promoting fair access to learning materials and closing the digital gap. They support the advancement of social justice and educational equity by making sure that all students, regardless of background or financial level, have access to top-notch media resources and technologies.

To sum up, the FTCE Educational Media Specialist exam is an essential part of the certification process for individuals who want to work as educational media specialists. It evaluates candidates' knowledge, abilities, and preparedness for this important position. In today's quickly changing educational landscape, the exam helps to guarantee that educational media experts are well-prepared to address the changing requirements of educators and students by upholding high standards of quality and encouraging continual professional development.

Chapter 2: Media Foundations for Education

Educational media foundations are firmly anchored in the theoretical, philosophical, and historical frameworks that have influenced the field throughout history. The development of educational media, well-known theories of learning and instructional design, and the ideas of digital and information literacy—which serve as the cornerstones of contemporary educational media practices—will all be covered in this chapter.

2.1 The Evolution of Educational Media Through History

The origins of educational media can be found in the ancient societies that used books, oral traditions, and crude teaching aids to spread knowledge. But the development of the printing press in the fifteenth century was a pivotal point in the democratization of knowledge, as it made it possible to produce and disseminate educational resources like books, pamphlets, and newspapers in large quantities.

Technological developments of the 20th century, including radio, film, television, and subsequently digital media, changed the field of educational media and allowed teachers to use a variety of multimedia resources to improve instruction. Educational media has continuously changed to accommodate the changing demands of students in a variety of educational contexts, starting with the introduction of instructional movies and audio recordings and continuing with the creation of interactive multimedia software and online learning platforms.

A wide range of formats, such as print materials, digital resources, audiovisual content, and interactive multimedia, are now included in instructional media, which reflects the expansion of information and communication technology and the interconnectedness of modern society.

2.2 Instructional Design and Learning Theories

Different learning and instructional design theories are fundamental to the field of educational media because they guide the creation and execution of media-rich learning experiences. These theories offer guidance for creating engaging learning activities and materials for students as well as frameworks for comprehending how students learn.

Behaviorism, which was developed by psychologists like Ivan Pavlov and B.F. Skinner, asserts that reward plays a major role in modifying behavior and that learning arises from correlations between stimuli and responses. Behaviorist ideas have shaped methods of designing instructional materials, including behavior modification and programmed teaching, which use media to create repeatable, structured learning experiences.

Researchers like Jean Piaget and Lev Vygotsky have espoused cognitivism, which highlights the importance of cognitive functions like memory, attention, and problem-solving in the learning process. This viewpoint holds that knowledge is actively constructed by students through mental processes like social interaction, information processing, and schema building. Instructional design frameworks like Merrill's First Principles of Instruction and Gagne's Nine Events of Instruction, which emphasize meaningful learning experiences through scaffolding, activation of existing knowledge, and strategic use of media, are informed by cognitive theories.

Constructivism is the theory that learning is a process of creating meaning and knowledge that is influenced by learners' past experiences, beliefs, and cultural surroundings. It is based on the work of educators such as John Dewey and Jerome Bruner. Constructivist methods support inquiry-based learning, collaborative problem-solving, and learner-centered education. Media are tools that support inquiry, discovery, and reflection.

The constructivist perspective is expanded upon by connectivism, which was put forth in the digital age by George Siemens and Stephen Downes. It includes the notion that learning is dispersed among networks of people, resources, and technologies. Through social media, online communities, and open educational resources, learners participate in knowledge creation and sharing in a networked learning environment. They use digital technology to access, assess, and remix material from a variety of sources.

Educational media specialists may create and provide media-rich learning experiences that cater to the varied requirements, preferences, and learning styles of students, encouraging engagement, motivation, and in-depth comprehension. They can achieve this by utilizing insights from various learning theories.

2.3 Knowledge of Technology and Information

Digital literacy and information literacy have become vital skills for navigating the digital world and assessing media content in an era marked by exponential expansion in digital information and rapid technical advancement.

The abilities, know-how, and mindset needed to use digital tools for critical thinking, communication, teamwork, and creativity are all included in digital literacy. Digitally literate people can use digital media tools and platforms ethically, traverse digital settings, and evaluate the veracity and credibility of online material. Among the essential elements of digital literacy are:

Technological competency is the ability to use computers, software, and internet resources for a variety of tasks, from simple ones like emailing and web browsing to more complex ones like coding and multimedia production. Information fluency is the ability to locate, assess, and combine material from digital sources, such as websites, databases, and online archives, to aid in research, learning, and decision-making.
Digital citizenship is the practice of acting morally and responsibly on the internet, which includes protecting privacy, upholding intellectual property rights, using social media in a responsible manner, and being safe online. Understanding the social, cultural, and political ramifications of media representations as well as identifying biases, prejudices, and propaganda tactics are all components of media literacy.
Contrarily, information literacy is the capacity to recognize, assess, and apply knowledge in order to solve issues, reach wise decisions, and pursue lifelong learning. People who are information literate can identify their information needs, find pertinent resources, assess information sources critically, and use information in an ethical manner to solve problems in the real world. Important elements of information literacy consist of:

Creating research questions, creating search plans, and utilizing a variety of resources—such as databases, online repositories, and libraries—to obtain information are all part of information seeking.
Information assessment is the process of evaluating the reliability, correctness, currency, and applicability of information sources using standards like objectivity, authority, and currency to help make well-informed decisions.
Information usage includes utilizing information to solve issues, make decisions, and effectively convey findings. It also involves integrating

information into knowledge frameworks and synthesizing various points of view.

Using information ethically involves upholding the rights to intellectual property, appropriately crediting sources, and using information in accordance with professional and academic ethics standards.

Educational media experts enable people to negotiate the intricacies of the digital age, critically assess media content, and become responsible, educated citizens in a world that is changing quickly by fostering digital literacy and information literacy abilities in students and educators.

In conclusion, the theoretical, philosophical, and historical pillars of educational media provide a rich tapestry that has influenced the discipline throughout history. Educational media specialists can effectively harness the power of media to enhance teaching and learning in the modern digital age by understanding the evolution of educational media, investigating well-known theories of learning and instructional design, and accepting digital literacy and information literacy as fundamental competencies.

Chapter 3: Resources and Media Technologies

In all educational contexts, the use of media technology and resources is essential for improving teaching and learning outcomes. This chapter will examine the wide range of media formats, tools, and resources that educators might use, from digital resources and interactive multimedia platforms to traditional print materials. We will look at the traits, advantages, and possible uses of a range of media technologies in addition to methods for successfully incorporating them into teaching methods.

3.1 Print Media: Newspapers, Magazines, and Books

Print media, which includes books, periodicals, and newspapers, has long been a mainstay in educational settings, offering students of all ages invaluable knowledge, inspiration, and information. Print media still has a big part in helping pupils develop their literacy, thinking critically, and developing a love of reading, even in the age of rapidly developing digital technologies.

Books are arguably the most common print medium in educational settings, providing a plethora of knowledge on a diverse variety of topics, genres, and forms. Books give teachers flexible tools for curriculum enrichment, differentiation, and individualized learning. These resources range from textbooks and reference materials to literature and fiction. Additionally, books take readers to other places, cultures, and viewpoints, stimulating their imagination, creativity, and empathy.

Because they provide up-to-date information on issues, trends, and events, magazines and newspapers present chances for media literacy, critical analysis, and interdisciplinary learning. Teachers can use magazines and newspapers to help students learn about media literacy, information literacy, and source evaluation while also including them in conversations about social justice, environmental sustainability, and global citizenship.

By exposing kids to a variety of viewpoints, cultures, and experiences, print media can help students develop a love of reading, encourage critical thinking, and broaden their horizons. Educators can leverage the potential of print media to spark curiosity, stimulate creativity, and develop lifelong learners by amassing an extensive library of print materials and offering chances for self-directed reading, guided conversations, and cooperative projects.

3.2 Digital Media: Social Media, Blogs, and Websites

Digital media technologies have revolutionized the way we create, access, and exchange information in the modern digital age, creating new opportunities for instruction and learning in educational settings. Digital media provides instructors with an abundance of resources for involving students, encouraging teamwork, and developing digital literacy abilities. These resources range from interactive websites and instructional blogs to social media platforms and online communities.

Websites are flexible tools that may be used to provide students in a variety of subject areas and grade levels with interactive activities, multimedia content, and educational resources. With access to educational resources, multimedia presentations, and interactive simulations that accommodate various learning preferences and styles, educational websites can work as virtual classrooms. Through the process of selecting and organizing a library of reputable websites, teachers can add value to their students' education, differentiate their teaching methods, and expand their classroom learning.

Teachers can now share ideas, resources, and comments on teaching and learning on a new platform: blogs. A vast range of subjects are covered by educational blogs, including professional development, technological integration, lesson plans, and teaching techniques. Teachers can start their own blogs to share student work, reflect on their experiences as educators, and interact with other educators and professionals in the area. Teachers can also encourage students to start their own blogs as a way for them to express themselves, think back on their education, and meaningfully interact with their classmates.

Social media sites like Facebook, Instagram, and Twitter give teachers the chance to engage in professional learning communities, exchange ideas and resources, and establish connections with kids, parents, and other educators. Social media can be used to highlight educational opportunities, give a voice to students, and start conversations about significant problems and subjects. Nonetheless, it is crucial that educators set an example for responsible and moral social media use, which includes upholding professional boundaries, respecting individuals' privacy, and critically analyzing content published online.

Teachers may build dynamic and engaging learning environments that promote teamwork, creativity, and critical thinking abilities by utilizing the power of digital media technology. Teachers may enhance their students' digital literacy abilities, engage students in real learning experiences, and set them up for success in a world that is changing quickly by including websites, blogs, and social media platforms into their lesson plans.

3.3 Audiovisual Content: Podcasts, Videos, and Interactive Displays

Teachers can communicate content, engage students, and improve learning experiences with the help of audiovisual media, such as interactive presentations, podcasts, and videos. Audiovisual materials that combine visual and aural components can draw in students with a variety of learning styles, hold their interest, and help them understand and remember important ideas.

Videos are useful tools that may be used to introduce new subjects, clarify difficult ideas, and give practical examples that make learning more relatable. Educational films are available in a variety of formats, such as tutorials, documentaries, and animations, and they cover a broad range of topics and disciplines. Teachers can utilize films to enhance curriculum materials, start conversations, and help students grasp important topics more deeply. Reputable sources for videos include educational publishers, museums, and websites like YouTube and Khan Academy.

A growing number of people are using podcasts to deliver educational content, giving students the chance to participate in audio-based conversations, interviews, and storytelling on a variety of subjects. Educational podcasts are a versatile and portable medium that educators can use to impart curriculum, encourage critical thinking, and promote digital literacy skills. They cover a wide range of disciplines, from science and history to literature and culture. Podcasts can be added to lesson plans by teachers as extra resources, exercises, or chances for individual study, giving students the freedom to delve further into subjects at their own pace.

Using multimedia slideshows and digital storytelling tools, educators may create dynamic and captivating learning experiences that promote active involvement and investigation through interactive presentations. Teachers may make presentations more visually appealing and dynamic, accommodate different learning styles, and encourage deeper engagement with the material by adding multimedia components including photographs, videos, audio clips, and interactive quizzes. Educators may easily create multimedia presentations that can be shared online, viewed remotely, and tailored to the needs of different learners with the use of tools like Google Slides, Prezi, and Adobe Spark.

Teachers can design immersive and engaging learning experiences that appeal to a varied student body, develop critical thinking abilities, and advance a deeper comprehension of important subjects by utilizing audiovisual media technology. By including interactive presentations, podcasts, and videos into their lesson plans, teachers may increase student participation, provide more access to material, and provide them the tools they need to take an active role in their own education.

3.4 Recap

To sum up, in the current educational landscape, media technologies and resources present educators with a multitude of chances to improve teaching and learning experiences. Media technologies offer instructors a range of tools to facilitate the delivery of curriculum, engage students, and develop critical thinking abilities. These tools include digital resources, interactive multimedia platforms, and traditional print materials. Print, digital, audiovisual, and interactive media can all be incorporated into instructional techniques to help educators build dynamic, inclusive learning environments that meet students' varied needs, preferences, and learning styles. It is critical for educational media professionals to be up to date on new developments in media technology, assess the value of media resources, and consistently look for chances for professional development. Through leveraging media technology and resources, educators may stimulate students' curiosity, fire their enthusiasm for learning, and equip them with the tools they need to flourish in a world that is changing quickly.

Chapter 4: Development and Management of Collections

A key part of the job description for an educational media expert is collection development and administration, which includes choosing, acquiring, organizing, and maintaining a variety of media materials to enhance instruction in a variety of learning environments. This chapter will cover criteria for assessing and choosing media materials, the concepts and practices of collection development and management, and methods for efficiently setting up and managing media collections to suit the needs of educators and students.

4.1 Selection Standards for Instructional Materials

The needs, interests, and learning objectives of educators and students must be carefully taken into account before any collection can be developed in an effective manner. Educational media experts must take into account a number of aspects while choosing media resources for the collection, such as community preferences, student demographics, curricular standards, and instructional objectives. Teachers can make sure that the collection is up to date, relevant, and supportive of learning objectives by matching media choices with curriculum priorities and learning objectives.

Important standards for assessing and choosing instructional media resources consist of:

Relevance of content: Educational frameworks and standards documents specify important concepts, subjects, and abilities that should be covered in media products. These resources should also be in line with curriculum standards, instructional objectives, and learning goals. To encourage inclusion and cultural responsiveness, materials should be up to date, accurate, and age-appropriate, reflecting a range of viewpoints, cultures, and experiences.

Pedagogical value: By providing chances for differentiation, enrichment, and extension, media products should accommodate a range of instructional techniques, learning styles, and student needs. To encourage active engagement, critical thinking, and inquiry-based learning, materials should be interesting, interactive, and easily available.

Credibility and quality: Professional production values, precise content, and a clear presentation are all necessary for high-quality media items. Reputable publishers, producers, and authors should supply the materials; accuracy, authority, and objectivity should be prioritized. Teachers should assess media sources critically for prejudice, misinformation, and stereotypes to make sure that the content respects cultural sensitivity and portrays a variety of viewpoints.

Accessibility and inclusivity: All students, regardless of their backgrounds, learning styles, or needs, should be able to use media resources. To accommodate varying learning styles, preferences, and sensory capacities, materials should be made available in a variety of forms and modalities. To guarantee diversity and equity, educators should take into account aspects including readability, language skill, and cultural relevance while choosing media resources.

Sustainability and cost-effectiveness: Media materials should maximize resources while reducing waste and their negative effects on the environment. In order to optimize resource allocation and support long-term sustainability, educators should take into account factors like licensing agreements, subscription costs, and digital rights management when choosing media materials. They should also investigate options for open educational resources (OER), free and inexpensive alternatives, and cooperative sharing arrangements.

Educational media professionals can create broad and inclusive collections that accommodate a wide range of instructional requirements and learning preferences by methodically and cooperatively implementing these selection criteria. Teachers can make sure that the collection is dynamic, responsive, and in line with changing curriculum priorities and learning objectives by conducting regular assessments and evaluations.

4.2 Purchasing and Planning

Educational media specialists must manage the budgeting and acquisitions processes to acquire, license, or buy the chosen media within the financial limits after they have been chosen for the collection. A number of procedures are involved in budgeting and acquisitions, such as locating funding sources, comparing prices, negotiating license terms, and effectively and openly overseeing purchasing procedures.

Important things to keep in mind when purchasing and budgeting are:

Funding sources: To support purchases, educational media experts need to determine whether sources of funding are available, such as grants, contributions, school or district budgets, and fundraising campaigns. Through cooperation with administrators, finance officers, and other relevant parties, educators can obtain sufficient financing to facilitate the achievement of collection development objectives and priorities.

Budget allocation: Within the limited financial limits, educational media professionals must carefully distribute budget resources, striking a balance between conflicting objectives and needs. Teachers can make the most of budgetary allocations by giving priority to materials that have a significant impact and are in line with curriculum standards, instructional objectives, and learning goals. This will guarantee that resources are distributed fairly and efficiently.

Price negotiations: To get advantageous terms and conditions for acquisitions, educational media specialists may bargain with suppliers, publishers, and producers about pricing and licensing arrangements. Educators can increase the purchasing power of available budget resources and optimize resource allocation by leveraging purchasing power, investigating bulk discounts, and pursuing competitive bids.

Collaboration and partnerships: To pool resources, split expenses, and obtain special pricing on media materials, educational media professionals might work with associates, consortia, and associations. Teachers can use their collective bargaining power to get preferential price and license terms, increase resource accessibility, and save costs by taking part in cooperative purchasing agreements, consortia purchasing initiatives, and group licensing arrangements.

Educational media experts can improve resource allocation, enhance purchasing power, and maximize the value and effect of the media collection by taking a strategic and collaborative approach to budgeting and acquisitions. Educators may maintain a collection that is responsive, robust, and in line with student needs and instructional priorities by using prudent budget planning, open and honest procurement procedures, and wise decision-making.

4.3 Systems for Cataloging and Classification

To make it easier for students and teachers to access, retrieve, and use media materials, educational media experts must methodically classify and catalog the materials after they have been purchased and added to the collection. Systems for cataloging and classifying media items offer a structure for arranging them based on genre, subject matter, format, and other characteristics, making it easier for users to find and access content quickly.

Important elements of systems for classification and cataloging include:

Descriptive metadata: Cataloging records have subject headers, keywords, and descriptive notes that give further context and details about the content and extent of the material. They also contain bibliographic data like title, author, publisher, publication date, and edition. Descriptive metadata makes it easier for consumers to find and assess media content by giving them access to pertinent features and properties.

Subject classification: Based on their subject matter and content, media materials are categorized using subject classification systems like the Library of Congress Classification (LCC) system and the Dewey Decimal Classification (DDC) system, which assign distinct call numbers or identifiers to each. Subject classification systems allow users to search and browse information within particular subject areas and disciplines by classifying materials into hierarchical categories and subcategories.

Access points: Author names, title keywords, subject headings, and other identifiers that let users search, browse, and retrieve contents from the collection are examples of access points included in cataloging records. Access points give users access to the collection through a variety of entrance points, enabling them to find content according to their preferences and many criteria, including authorship, subject matter, or genre.

Authority control: To guarantee accuracy and consistency in the names, terminology, and subjects represented throughout the collection, cataloging records may incorporate authority control procedures. Authority control improves the coherence and usability of the cataloging system by standardizing access points, resolving spelling or terminology variances, and establishing linkages between related content.

Educational media specialists can arrange media resources so that students and teachers can access, retrieve, and use them more easily by using systematic and consistent categorization and classification methods. Teachers can maximize resource discovery, expedite information access, and encourage the efficient use of media materials to meet teaching and learning objectives by implementing good cataloging procedures.

4.4 Recap

To sum up, collection development and management—which include the choice, purchase, arrangement, and upkeep of a variety of media materials to enhance teaching and learning in a variety of educational settings—are crucial components of the work of an educational media specialist. Through the methodical use of evaluation and selection criteria, educators can create collections of media materials that are comprehensive, current, and in line with the needs of their students as well as instructional priorities. Teachers may make the most use of their purchasing power, allocate resources efficiently, and maintain a collection that is responsive, robust, and in line with curriculum standards and learning objectives by strategically planning their budgets and acquisitions. Educators can promote the efficient use of media materials to support teaching and learning objectives, make resource search and retrieval easier, and organize media materials systematically by implementing cataloging and classification systems. It is critical for educational media experts to remain up to date on new developments in collection building and management, assess the efficacy of cataloging procedures, and persistently look for chances to further their careers. By adopting best practices for collection building and maintenance, educators may produce inclusive, dynamic media collections that ignite students' curiosity, encourage participation, and equip them for success in a world that is changing quickly.

Chapter 5: Design and Delivery of Instruction

The core responsibilities of educational media experts include instructional design and delivery, which entails the methodical preparation, creation, and execution of media-rich learning experiences to enhance teaching and learning in a variety of educational contexts. This chapter will cover the fundamental ideas and methods of instructional design, as well as important models and techniques. It will also go over practical methods for incorporating instructional media into practices that will improve student engagement, understanding, and retention of important concepts.

5.1 Comprehending Instructional Design

The methodical process of developing successful and captivating learning environments that encourage student motivation, engagement, and accomplishment is known as instructional design. Instructional design, which has its roots in educational psychology and learning theories, places a strong emphasis on how important it is to match learners' needs and preferences with learning objectives, instructional methodologies, and assessment techniques.

Important elements of instructional design consist of:

Analysis: A detailed examination of the needs, traits, and past knowledge of the learners as well as the educational goals, objectives, and limitations forms the basis of instructional design. Teachers may create engaging, relevant, and accessible learning experiences by getting to know their students' interests, backgrounds, and learning styles.

Design: Teachers create educational resources, exercises, and tests that support learning objectives and instructional goals during this stage. Choosing media formats, creating interactive exercises, and creating evaluations that track students' development and performance are examples of design decisions.

Development: To support learning objectives and instructional activities, educators generate and produce educational materials, multimedia resources, and interactive aspects during the development phase. Development can entail producing interactive simulations, digitizing content, making films, or selecting already-existing media materials for educational use.

Implementation: Teachers carry out the lesson plan by giving students instruction and supervising their learning activities in a classroom or online setting after the instructional materials have been created. Students must participate in active learning activities, receive encouragement and feedback, and have their involvement and progress tracked.

Evaluation: Students' and stakeholders' input is gathered, instructional materials and learning experiences are evaluated for their efficacy, and modifications are made in response to formative and summative assessment results. Analyzing student performance, evaluating learning objectives, and considering teaching methods in order to guide future adjustments and enhancements are some examples of evaluation tasks.

Teachers can build successful learning experiences that enhance student learning and accomplishment by using a methodical, iterative approach to instructional design.

5.2 Models of Instructional Design

A number of paradigms for instructional design offer structures and principles for creating and executing learning experiences that are rich in media. These models provide organized methods for organizing, creating, and presenting teaching. They place special focus on matching instructional methodologies, learning objectives, and evaluation techniques to meet the requirements and preferences of the students.

Several well-known models of instructional design include:

ADDIE Model: A popular framework for creating educational resources and learning experiences is the ADDIE (Analysis, Design, Development, Implementation, and Evaluation) model. In order to generate successful and captivating learning experiences, the ADDIE model places an emphasis on a methodical approach to instructional design that involves iterative cycles of analysis, design, development, implementation, and evaluation.

SAM Model: Focused on fast prototype, feedback, and iteration, the SAM (Successful Approximation Model) model is an iterative instructional design approach. The SAM model allows for flexibility and response to learner needs and input throughout the design and development process by breaking the instructional design process into iterative cycles of prototype, review, and modification.

Bloom's Taxonomy is a hierarchical framework that may be used to categorize learning objectives and cognitive processes. It can be applied to higher-order cognitive skills like applying, analyzing, evaluating, and creating, as well as lower-order cognitive skills like remembering and understanding. Teachers can create educational activities and assessments that target particular cognitive processes and complexity levels using an organized framework that is provided by Bloom's Taxonomy.

The nine instructional events or procedures for creating and delivering successful education are outlined in Gagne's Nine Events of education, a methodical approach to instructional design. These activities involve drawing students' attention, outlining goals, encouraging memory of previously learned material, delivering the lesson, offering learning assistance, eliciting performance, giving feedback, evaluating performance, and improving retention and transfer. Gagne's Nine Events of Instruction offer educators a methodical structure for organizing learning activities and fostering successful student outcomes.

Instructors can construct effective and engaging learning experiences that enhance student learning and achievement by employing instructional design concepts in a methodical and flexible manner.

5.3 Including Media Education in the Curriculum

When it comes to incorporating educational media into curricula to improve teaching and learning, educational media specialists are essential. Teachers can engage students in meaningful learning experiences, develop critical thinking abilities, and encourage active involvement and inquiry-based learning by utilizing a wide range of media resources, such as print materials, digital media, audiovisual content, and interactive multimedia.

Important methods for including instructional media in curricula include:

Curriculum standards, instructional goals, and learning objectives should all be taken into consideration when choosing and incorporating educational media within the curriculum. The content of the curriculum should be supported and enhanced by media assets, giving students the chance to apply skills, investigate important ideas, and participate in real-world learning opportunities.

Differentiating instruction: Learners' varied needs and preferences can be met by using educational media to differentiate instruction. Teachers can accommodate a variety of learning styles, interests, and skill levels by offering a variety of media options, such as text-based materials, multimedia resources, and interactive exercises.

Encouraging inquiry-based learning: By giving students the chance to autonomously explore, research, and find information, educational media can help encourage inquiry-based learning. Teachers have the ability to create media-rich learning environments that inspire students to think critically, ask questions, and look for answers.

Encouraging cooperation and communication: Students can cooperate to solve problems, exchange ideas, and produce multimedia projects when they have access to educational media. Teachers can use digital tools and platforms to facilitate communication and teamwork among students by implementing cooperative activities including group discussions, peer reviews, and cooperative projects.

Giving feedback and assessment: Teachers can monitor student progress, evaluate learning objectives, and promptly deliver feedback on students' performance by using educational media to give students feedback and assessments. Teachers can create interactive tests, quizzes, and multimedia presentations that provide students instant feedback and help them make judgments about how best to teach.

Education professionals may design effective and engaging learning experiences that enhance student learning and accomplishment by skillfully incorporating instructional media into the curriculum. When it comes to choosing, incorporating, and utilizing media resources to improve instruction in a variety of educational contexts, educational media professionals are indispensable.

5.4 Recap

In summary, the planning, creation, and execution of media-rich learning experiences in a methodical manner to facilitate teaching and learning in a variety of educational contexts constitute crucial components of the job description of an educational media specialist. Through the use of a methodical and iterative process for instructional design, educators may produce compelling and productive learning environments that foster motivation, achievement, and student engagement. Teachers can create and deliver media-rich learning experiences that meet curriculum standards, instructional goals, and learning objectives by utilizing instructional design models and methodologies. Education professionals may design effective and engaging learning experiences that enhance student learning and accomplishment by skillfully incorporating instructional media into the curriculum. It is critical for educational media experts to remain up to date on new developments in instructional design and delivery, assess the efficacy of instructional strategies, and persistently look for chances for professional development. Teachers may build vibrant, inclusive learning environments that stimulate curiosity, encourage engagement, and equip students to flourish in a world that is changing quickly by adopting best practices in instructional design and delivery.

Chapter 6: Ethics and Media Literacy

In the current digital era, media literacy and ethics are crucial skills for navigating the complicated media ecosystem. The significance of media literacy and ethics in educational contexts will be examined in this chapter, along with important media literacy ideas and abilities. Additionally, ways for encouraging students and educators to use media responsibly and ethically will be covered.

6.1 Grasping the Concept of Media Literacy

The ability to critically and effectively access, analyze, assess, and generate media content is referred to as media literacy. Media literacy is becoming more and more crucial for students to acquire the critical thinking abilities required for responsible citizenship and to navigate the vast amount of information that is available to them in an era marked by the growth of fake news and misinformation as well as the proliferation of digital media platforms.

Important elements of media literacy consist of:

Critical analysis: Being media literate entails being able to assess the veracity and credibility of sources, recognize biases, stereotypes, and disinformation in media messages. Students get a greater grasp of media material and its potential influence by learning to ask questions such who generated the message, what tactics were utilized to convey the message, and why the message was produced.

Media production: The capacity to produce media content in an ethical and responsible manner is another aspect of media literacy. Students gain knowledge of how to apply media production principles, including choosing suitable media formats, making efficient use of digital tools and technology, and abiding by moral standards and copyright regulations. Students gain communication, creative, and digital citizenship skills through media creation activities, enabling them to take an active role in the media landscape.

Digital citizenship: The idea of digital citizenship, which is the responsible, moral, and secure use of digital technologies and online platforms, is included in media literacy. Pupils gain knowledge on how to interact critically and ethically with digital media, upholding the rights of intellectual property, safeguarding personal data, and making valuable contributions to online communities. Teachers can enable children to navigate the digital world with confidence and ethics by fostering digital citizenship abilities.

Information literacy: The ability to find, assess, and use information effectively to solve issues, make decisions, and convey findings is strongly related to media literacy. In order to make well-informed decisions, students must be able to critically analyze information, discern between fact and opinion, and evaluate the authority and dependability of sources. Students who master information literacy become astute media producers and consumers, able to handle the intricacies of the information era.

6.2 Encouraging Media Literacy in Learning Environments

By including media literacy instruction into curricula and giving students the chance to interact critically with media information, educators may help students develop their media literacy abilities. Teachers can assist students in developing the information, abilities, and attitudes required to successfully navigate the media world by adding media literacy exercises, conversations, and projects into their lessons.

Important tactics for encouraging media literacy in learning environments consist of:

Media analysis: By looking at commercials, news stories, websites, and other media sources, educators can help students analyze media messages critically. In addition to learning how to recognize persuasive strategies, examine framing and bias, and assess the validity and dependability of sources, students also gain critical thinking and media literacy skills.

Media production: Using digital tools and technology, educators can provide students the chance to produce their own media output, including podcasts, videos, and digital presentations. Students learn digital literacy, communication, and creative thinking abilities as well as the ethical obligations and concerns of media producers through participation in media creation activities.

Digital citizenship education: To encourage the ethical and responsible use of digital technology and online platforms, educators can incorporate digital citizenship education into their curricula. Students study topics including cyberbullying, privacy, security, and online manners. They also investigate methods for successfully resolving digital obstacles and problems. Teachers can enable students to utilize digital media responsibly and ethically in both their personal and academic lives by promoting a culture of digital citizenship.

Teaching pupils how to seek, assess, and use information effectively to enhance learning and decision-making is one of the many information literacy abilities that educators may impart to their students. Students gain knowledge about how to evaluate the authority and dependability of sources, appropriately reference material, and apply moral standards when utilizing it. Students who acquire information literacy skills become critical information producers and consumers, able to handle the complexity of the digital information environment.

By incorporating media literacy instruction into the curriculum and giving students the chance to interact critically with media, teachers can enable their students to become knowledgeable, ethical, and responsible media consumers and creators.

6.3 Comprehending Media Ethics

The values and norms of behavior that direct the moral behavior of media professionals, such as writers, filmmakers, and content producers, are referred to as media ethics. Truthfulness, accuracy, justice, privacy, and transparency are just a few of the ethical issues that are covered by media ethics, which also highlights the significance of maintaining moral principles throughout the creation and dissemination of media.

Among the fundamentals of media ethics are:

Accuracy and truthfulness: It is the duty of media professionals to report on the news with integrity, avoiding factual errors, distortions, and misrepresentations. Maintaining the legitimacy and dependability of media sources and fostering educated public discourse depend on accurate reporting.

Fairness and balance: Media workers should make an effort to convey information in an unbiased and fair manner, giving a range of viewpoints and offering impartial coverage of topics and events. presenting voice to all sides of a subject, avoiding bias and prejudice, and presenting context and background information to assist people understand complicated issues are all necessary for fair reporting.

Privacy and consent: Before utilizing a person's name or image in media content, media professionals should respect that person's right to privacy and get that person's informed consent. Protecting private information, upholding personal space, and refraining from invasive or exploitative actions that could violate someone's dignity or privacy are all important privacy considerations.

Accountability and transparency: Journalists should be open and honest about their sources, techniques, and goals. They should also declare any conflicts of interest and prejudices that can have an impact on their reporting. Transparency ensures that media practitioners follow ethical standards and principles and fosters responsibility in media practices. It also creates confidence and credibility with audiences.

Social responsibility: It is the duty of media professionals to uphold the public interest and support an educated and well-informed democratic society. In addition to addressing matters of public importance in a responsible and ethical manner, media material should encourage civic involvement, social justice, and democratic values.

6.4 Encouraging Media Ethics in Learning Environments

By include ethical issues into media literacy instruction and giving students the chance to investigate moral conundrums and the decision-making processes involved in the creation and consumption of media, educators can significantly contribute to the promotion of media ethics among their students. Teachers can enable students to appropriately and ethically navigate the intricacies of the media ecosystem by cultivating ethical awareness and critical thinking abilities.

The following are important tactics for advancing media ethics in learning environments:

Talks about ethics in media production and consumption: Teachers can lead talks on ethical issues in media production and consumption, covering subjects like transparency, privacy, truthfulness, and justice. By discussing ethical conundrums and the processes involved in making decisions in the creation and dissemination of media, students gain the ability to critically assess media content in the context of moral principles and values.

Case studies and scenarios: These can be used by educators to demonstrate moral conundrums and the decision-making processes involved in the creation and consumption of media. Students examine real-world instances of moral failings and media disputes, taking into account the ramifications for people as a whole, society at large, and democratic government. Students gain ethical awareness and critical thinking abilities through the analysis of case studies and scenarios, which equips them to successfully negotiate moral dilemmas in the media environment.

Media production projects: Instructors can provide students the chance to produce their own digital presentations, podcasts, and films while emphasizing ethical obligations and considerations. While producing media, students are taught to apply ethical concepts and values, taking into account concerns like accuracy, fairness, privacy, and openness. Students who participate in media production projects learn about the moral difficulties involved in the creation and dissemination of media, enabling them to make moral decisions both as media creators and viewers.

Experts and guest speakers: Teachers might ask professionals in the media, like journalists, filmmakers, and content developers, to give their thoughts and ideas on professional conduct and media ethics. The experiences and examples from the actual world shared by the guest speakers offer insightful perspectives on the moral obligations and difficulties faced by media workers. Students learn more about media ethics and how it relates to their own lives and communities by interacting with professionals and guest speakers.

By including media ethics education into the curriculum and giving students the chance to investigate moral conundrums and the processes involved in producing and consuming media, educators may provide students with the skills they need to responsibly and ethically navigate the complex media world.

6.5 Recap

To sum up, in the current digital era, media literacy and ethics are critical skills for negotiating the complicated media ecosystem. Teachers may enable students to access, analyze, evaluate, and produce media content critically and effectively by fostering media literacy abilities. This will allow students to navigate the media ecosystem with confidence and discernment. Teachers can enable students to properly and ethically negotiate ethical difficulties in media creation and consumption, so contributing to a well-informed and robust democratic society, by cultivating ethical awareness and critical thinking abilities. As media experts in education, we must incorporate media literacy and ethics instruction into curricula, give students the chance to interact critically with media, and develop their capacity for moral judgment in both the creation and consumption of media. Teachers may enable students to become knowledgeable, accountable, and moral media consumers and creators who can confidently and honorably negotiate the intricacies of the media ecosystem by adopting media literacy and ethics teaching.

Chapter 7: Cooperation and Career Advancement

In order to promote a culture of cooperation, innovation, and ongoing learning among educators and stakeholders, professional development and collaboration are crucial aspects of the job of an educational media specialist. The significance of collaboration and professional development in educational settings will be examined in this chapter, along with important tactics and approaches for promoting these qualities. Additionally, the role of educational media specialists in assisting collaborative initiatives and professional learning communities will be covered.

7.1 The Value of Teamwork in Educational Environments

In educational environments, collaboration is essential for improving teaching techniques, supporting student performance, and creating a culture of continual development. Educators may address the different needs of students, foster creativity, and accomplish common goals and objectives by collaborating with colleagues, administrators, parents, and community stakeholders. This allows them to use their collective skills, resources, and views.

Several advantages of teamwork in learning environments include:

Improved learning opportunities: Through collaboration, instructors can exchange materials, teaching strategies, and best practices, which benefits students' learning and fosters interdisciplinary connections. Educators may create integrated and authentic learning experiences that engage students in meaningful ways and foster better knowledge of essential concepts by working with colleagues from other disciplines and backgrounds.

Professional development: Working together gives educators the chance to exchange knowledge and experiences, reflect on their work, and learn from one another. Through engagement in cooperative endeavors like mentorship programs, peer observations, and professional learning communities, educators can enhance their expertise and abilities, obtain constructive criticism and assistance, and consistently refine their teaching methodologies.

Improved academic outcomes and increased student accomplishment have been associated with instructor collaboration. Teachers may address learning gaps, provide focused interventions, and support every student's academic performance by collaborating to assess student data, identify instructional needs, and adopt evidence-based practices.

Building a collaborative school culture: Teachers who collaborate with one another have a greater sense of community, shared responsibility, and respect for one another. This leads to the development of a supportive school culture that emphasizes cooperation, teamwork, and ongoing improvement. Through cultivating constructive relationships and cooperative alliances, educators may establish a learning atmosphere in which every student feels appreciated, encouraged, and equipped for success.

7.2 Techniques for Promoting Teamwork

By supporting collaborative projects, offering resources and assistance, and encouraging a collaborative and innovative culture, educational media specialists play a critical role in increasing collaboration among educators. By putting collaborative learning ideas into practice, educators may take advantage of their group knowledge and assets to boost student achievement and accomplish common goals and objectives.

Important tactics for encouraging cooperation among teachers are as follows:

Forming professional learning communities (PLCs): PLCs bring together teachers from many disciplines and grade levels to discuss best practices, examine student data, and work collaboratively on instructional strategies. PLCs give teachers the chance to participate in group problem-solving, introspection, and professional development, which promotes an innovative and continuous improvement culture.

Organizing interdisciplinary projects, units, and initiatives that incorporate several topic areas and foster linkages between disciplines is one way that educational media professionals can support cross-disciplinary collaboration. Teachers can create integrated and realistic learning experiences that meaningfully engage students and foster a deeper understanding of important concepts by working with colleagues from many disciplines.

Offering opportunities for professional development: Educational media professionals can offer training sessions, seminars, and workshops that center on technology integration, instructional methodologies, and collaborative practices. Instructing educators with the information, abilities, and tools necessary for productive teamwork can help them cultivate a collaborative and innovative culture in learning environments.

Promoting collaboration between educators and students through technology integration: Educational media professionals are able to assist with technology integration initiatives. Educators may foster creative educational practices and improve stakeholder engagement by giving them access to digital tools, resources, and platforms that promote communication, sharing of ideas, and collaboration.

Encouraging educators to participate in decision-making processes such as curriculum development, resource allocation, and school improvement planning is one way that educational media specialists can encourage educators to take on a shared leadership and decision-making role. In order to promote a sense of accountability, ownership, and dedication to common goals and objectives, educators should be given the freedom to bring their knowledge and viewpoints to decision-making processes.

Educational media specialists can enhance student performance and accomplish shared goals and objectives in educational environments by putting techniques into place that encourage collaboration among educators. By doing so, they can take advantage of their collective skills, resources, and views.

7.3 The Value of Continuing Education

To stay up to date on new developments in the field of education, improve their knowledge and abilities, and adjust to evolving teaching methods and technological advancements, educators must engage in professional development. Teachers can enhance student learning, enhance their own teaching strategies, and promote a continuous improvement culture in the classroom by taking part in professional development events.

Among the main advantages of professional development for teachers are:

Improving teaching methods: Through professional development, teachers can acquire new techniques, tools, and tactics that can improve student involvement, understanding, and performance. Educators can broaden their teaching repertoire, integrate evidence-based approaches, and customize instruction to cater to the varied needs and preferences of students by engaging in professional development events.

Keeping up with trends in education: Through professional development, teachers can remain up to date on new developments in the field, including technological advancements, pedagogical approaches, and scientific discoveries. Educators can ensure that their teaching remains successful and relevant in a fast changing educational context by remaining up to date on current advancements in the area and adapting their instructional strategies to reflect best practices and evidence-based approaches.

Promoting networking and collaboration: Professional development gives educators the chance to work together, exchange resources and ideas, and establish professional networks. Engaging in professional development activities allows educators to establish connections with mentors, colleagues, and subject matter experts. This promotes a collaborative, innovative, and ongoing learning culture within educational environments.

Encouraging reflective practice: Teachers are urged by professional development to reflect on their teaching methods, evaluate their methods, evaluate the learning objectives of their students, and pinpoint areas in which they may still grow and improve. Teachers who reflect on their teaching experiences can pinpoint their professional growth objectives, pinpoint their areas of strength and weakness, and make well-informed decisions that will improve their teaching methods and help students learn.

7.4 Professional Development Techniques

Professional development for educators is greatly aided by educational media professionals, who offer training sessions, tools, and encouragement of an ongoing culture of learning and development. Through the use of professional development initiatives, educators can improve their knowledge and abilities, facilitate student learning, and foster an innovative and excellence-focused culture within educational environments.

Important tactics for encouraging educators' professional growth include:

Accessing resources and materials: Educational media specialists can facilitate professional growth by connecting people with books, articles, videos, and online courses, among other resources, materials, and online platforms. Educators can enable their colleagues to investigate novel concepts, innovative technology, and pedagogical approaches while improving their professional expertise by selecting and sharing pertinent resources.

Professional learning communities, training sessions, and workshops on important subjects and topics of interest to educators, like technology integration, literacy teaching, and assessment techniques, can be facilitated by educational media specialists. Through practical guidance, opportunities for collaboration, and hands-on experience, instructors can improve their methods of instruction and successfully support students' learning.

Mentoring and coaching: Educational media specialists can assist educators with mentoring and coaching, giving tailored advice, criticism, and encouragement to help peers enhance their teaching methods and reach their career objectives. Teachers can promote a climate of cooperation, development, and ongoing improvement in classrooms by acting as mentors and coaches.

Fostering a culture of innovation and excellence among educators and professional development: Educational media professionals have the ability to assist collaborative projects and initiatives. Teachers can participate in collaborative problem-solving, reflection, and professional growth by setting up interdisciplinary projects, action research initiatives, and collaborative learning communities. This will improve their knowledge and abilities and help students succeed.

Promoting reflective practice: By offering chances for self-evaluation, goal-setting, and reflection on instructional strategies and student learning results, educational media specialists can motivate teachers to participate in reflective practice. Educators can promote a culture of ongoing learning and development in educational environments by encouraging colleagues to reflect on their teaching experiences, identify areas for growth and improvement, and set goals for professional development.

Educational media specialists can help teachers improve their knowledge and abilities, aid in students' learning, and foster an innovative and high-achieving culture in classrooms by putting professional development ideas into practice.

7.5 Recap

To sum up, in order to promote a culture of cooperation, innovation, and ongoing learning among educators and stakeholders, professional development and collaboration are crucial aspects of the work of an educational media specialist. Through the promotion of collaboration among educators, educational media professionals can effectively utilize their combined knowledge, assets, and viewpoints to facilitate student achievement and accomplish common goals and objectives within educational environments. Educational media specialists can enable teachers to improve their knowledge and abilities, assist students in their learning, and foster an innovative and high-achieving culture in classrooms by providing chances for professional development. Facilitating collaborative projects, offering resources and assistance, and encouraging a culture of collaboration and professional development among educators are all critical tasks for educational media experts. Educators can increase student learning, improve their instructional techniques, and foster an excellence and continuous improvement culture in their educational environments by embracing cooperation and professional development.

Chapter 8: Evaluation and Assessment

The educational process is not complete without assessment and evaluation, which give teachers important information on student learning, the efficacy of their instruction, and the results of their programs. This chapter will cover the significance of assessment and evaluation in educational settings, as well as important assessment and evaluation practices and principles. It will also cover strategies for developing and putting into practice efficient methods of assessment and evaluation that will promote student success and guide instructional decision-making.

8.1 The Value of Assessment and Appraisal

In educational contexts, assessment and evaluation are essential for advancing student learning, directing instructional decision-making, and encouraging ongoing progress. Teachers can identify areas for improvement, customize instruction to match the requirements of individual students, and make sure that educational goals and objectives are successfully reached by methodically monitoring student progress, reviewing program results, and assessing instructional effectiveness.

In educational environments, assessment and evaluation are crucial for the following main reasons:

Educators can discover areas of strength and weakness, customize training to match the requirements of each individual student, and make well-informed decisions about their teaching by using the important data and insights that assessment and evaluation provide. Teachers can determine which teaching tactics are working and where further help or intervention might be required to assist students' learning by examining assessment data.

Encouraging student success: In order to help students succeed academically, instructors can track students' progress, spot learning gaps, and give timely feedback and assistance by using assessment and evaluation. Educators can effectively address students' learning needs by identifying areas where they may require further help or intervention through regular assessments of student learning outcomes and performance feedback. This allows educators to deliver tailored instruction in those areas.

Supporting program improvement: By giving educators information about the success of initiatives, programs, and interventions in education, evaluation helps them to pinpoint areas in need of development, hone programmatic goals and objectives, and make data-driven choices that will increase program efficacy. Teachers may make sure that resources are utilized wisely and that program goals and objectives are successfully accomplished by conducting a systematic evaluation of program outcomes.

Encouraging transparency and accountability: By informing stakeholders about programmatic impact, instructional efficacy, and student learning outcomes, assessment and evaluation help to foster transparency and accountability in education. Educators can communicate progress and accomplishments to stakeholders, such as parents, administrators, and legislators, and show the efficacy of their teaching techniques by gathering and evaluating assessment data.

8.2 Assessment and Evaluation Principles

Important guidelines and standards that guarantee fairness, validity, dependability, and transparency in the assessment process serve as a roadmap for efficient assessment and evaluation procedures. Educators can create and execute assessment and evaluation strategies that yield precise and significant data regarding student learning, program outcomes, and instructional efficacy by following these guidelines.

Among the fundamentals of assessment and evaluation are:

Alignment with learning objectives: To make sure that assessment and evaluation techniques measure the knowledge and skills that students should possess, they should be in line with curriculum standards, instructional goals, and learning objectives. Teachers may make sure that assessment results give useful information about student learning and accomplishment by matching tests with learning objectives.

Validity: Techniques for assessment and evaluation must reliably measure the desired learning outcomes and offer trustworthy data on the knowledge and abilities of students. Valid assessments measure pertinent knowledge and abilities, are founded on reliable assessment methods, and offer precise and insightful data regarding student performance.

Reliability: Techniques for assessment and evaluation should be able to yield consistent results over an extended period of time and with various administrations. When given to the same group of students in identical circumstances, reliable assessments produce consistent scores and offer a solid indicator of student achievement.

Fairness: Methods of assessment and evaluation should be equal and fair, which means that no student group should be unfairly benefited or harmed by them depending on characteristics like gender, race, socioeconomic status, or disability. Fair assessments are devoid of prejudice and discrimination, giving every student an equal chance to display their knowledge and abilities.

Transparency: Students, parents, teachers, and other stakeholders should be informed in a clear and understandable manner about the assessment and evaluation procedures. Transparent evaluations give students precise objectives, guidelines, and feedback, empowering them to see their areas of strength and growth and make wise decisions regarding their education.

8.3 Techniques for Efficient Assessment and Appraisal

In order to promote student achievement and provide information for instructional decision-making, educational media specialists are essential in the development and application of efficient assessment and evaluation techniques. Teachers can obtain precise and significant data regarding program outcomes, student learning, and instructional efficacy by putting effective assessment and evaluation procedures into practice. They can then utilize this data to inform instructional practice and support student achievement.

The following are crucial tactics for creating and putting into practice efficient assessment and evaluation procedures:

Assessment and evaluation techniques should be coordinated with curriculum standards, learning objectives, and instructional goals in order to measure the knowledge and skills that students should be able to demonstrate. Teachers may make sure that assessment results give useful information about student learning and accomplishment by matching tests with learning objectives.

Using a range of assessment techniques: To understand more about students' learning, teachers should employ a range of assessment techniques and instruments, such as formative, summative, performance-based, and authentic assessments. Teachers are able to compile a multitude of sources of information regarding students' learning and present a complete picture of their performance by employing an array of assessment techniques.

Giving prompt and helpful feedback: Teachers should provide students prompt and helpful feedback on their performance so they can identify their areas of strength and growth and make wise learning decisions. Effectively supporting students' growth and accomplishment can be achieved by educators through the provision of feedback that is targeted, practical, and integrated with learning objectives.

Engaging students in the evaluation process: Teachers should engage students in the evaluation process by offering chances for introspection on their learning, peer evaluation, and self-evaluation. Teachers can encourage metacognitive awareness, self-regulation, and ownership of learning by incorporating students in the evaluation process. This will enable students to participate actively in their education.

Instructional decision-making, identification of areas of strength and weakness, and adaptation of instructional techniques to meet the needs of individual students should all be informed by assessment data, according to educators. Teachers can spot trends and patterns in their students' performance, focus on areas where they might need more help or intervention, and modify their lesson plans by methodically evaluating assessment data.

Program outcomes evaluation: Teachers should systematically analyze program outcomes in order to determine the efficacy of initiatives, programs, and interventions in education. They should also make data-driven decisions in order to maximize the effectiveness of their programs. In order to increase program effectiveness and promote student achievement, educators can pinpoint areas for improvement, hone programmatic goals and objectives, and make evidence-based decisions by gathering and evaluating data on program outcomes.

Educational media specialists can collect precise and insightful data about student learning, program outcomes, and instructional effectiveness by putting effective assessment and evaluation strategies into practice. They can then use this data to inform instructional practice, encourage student success, and support ongoing improvement in educational settings.

Conclusion (8.4)

To sum up, assessment and evaluation are essential parts of the learning process because they give teachers important information on how well their lessons are being taught, how well their students are learning, and the results of their programs. Educators can guide instructional practice, promote student success, and foster continuous improvement in educational settings by developing and implementing efficient assessment and evaluation methods. By doing so, they can collect accurate and meaningful data about student learning, instructional effectiveness, and program outcomes. It is imperative that educational media specialists follow the fundamental guidelines and standards of assessment and evaluation, use a range of assessment techniques, match assessments to learning goals, give prompt, helpful feedback, involve students in the assessment process, and use assessment results to inform instruction and assess program outcomes. Educational media experts can enhance student performance, inform instructional decision-making, and contribute to a culture of excellence and continuous improvement in educational settings by putting good assessment and evaluation methodologies into practice.

Practice Questions and Answers Explanations 2024-2025

Question 1:

Which of the following best describes the purpose of media literacy education?

A) To promote uncritical consumption of media content
B) To develop critical thinking skills for analyzing media messages
C) To encourage students to believe everything they see in the media
D) To discourage students from engaging with media content

Answer: B)

Explanation: Media literacy education aims to develop critical thinking skills that enable individuals to analyze, evaluate, and understand media messages critically. It empowers students to navigate the complexities of the media landscape and make informed judgments about media content.

Question 2:

What is the primary focus of instructional design in educational media?

A) Creating visually appealing content
B) Aligning content with state standards
C) Meeting the diverse needs of learners
D) Incorporating the latest technology trends

Answer: C)

Explanation: The primary focus of instructional design in educational media is to meet the diverse needs of learners by designing content and resources that are accessible, engaging, and effective for all students, regardless of their backgrounds or learning styles.

Question 3:

Which of the following is a key consideration in collection development and management for educational media specialists?

A) Acquiring materials solely based on personal preferences
B) Ignoring copyright laws and fair use guidelines
C) Balancing diverse perspectives and viewpoints
D) Limiting access to resources for students

Answer: C)

Explanation: Collection development and management involve balancing diverse perspectives and viewpoints to ensure that the collection reflects the needs and interests of all students. Educational media specialists should strive to provide access to a wide range of materials that represent different cultural backgrounds, viewpoints, and experiences.

Question 4:

What is the purpose of scaffolding in instructional design?

A) To make content more challenging for advanced learners

B) To provide support and guidance to learners as they develop new skills

C) To remove all support and allow learners to work independently

D) To limit access to resources for struggling learners

Answer: B)

Explanation: Scaffolding in instructional design involves providing support and guidance to learners as they develop new skills or concepts. It helps learners build on their existing knowledge and abilities, gradually increasing complexity and independence over time.

Question 5:

Which of the following best describes the concept of media convergence?

A) The idea that media content should remain separate and distinct

B) The integration of multiple forms of media into a single platform

C) The decline of traditional media formats in favor of digital media

D) The censorship of media content by regulatory authorities

Answer: B)

Explanation: Media convergence refers to the integration of multiple forms of media, such as text, audio, video, and interactive elements, into a single platform or device. It allows users to access and interact with media content in new and innovative ways.

Question 6:

Which of the following is an example of an authentic assessment?

A) Multiple-choice test

B) Essay exam

C) Portfolio review

D) True/false quiz

Answer: C)

Explanation: A portfolio review is an example of an authentic assessment that allows students to demonstrate their knowledge, skills, and abilities in a real-world context by showcasing their work samples, projects, and accomplishments.

Question 7:

What is the purpose of copyright law in relation to educational media?
A) To restrict access to educational materials
B) To protect the rights of creators and authors
C) To prevent educators from using media content in the classroom
D) To limit the use of digital technologies in education

Answer: B)

Explanation: Copyright law aims to protect the rights of creators and authors by granting them exclusive rights to their original works, such as books, videos, and music. It establishes legal frameworks for the use and distribution of copyrighted materials, including fair use provisions that allow limited use of copyrighted materials for educational purposes.

Question 8:

Which of the following is an example of a formative assessment?
A) Final exam
B) Midterm project
C) Homework assignment
D) Classroom discussion

Answer: C)

Explanation: A homework assignment is an example of a formative assessment that provides ongoing feedback and support to students as they progress through a unit or course. Formative assessments help educators monitor student learning and adjust instruction accordingly.

Question 9:

What is the primary goal of media literacy education?
A) To promote passive consumption of media content
B) To develop critical thinking skills for analyzing media messages
C) To discourage students from engaging with media content
D) To limit access to media resources in educational settings

Answer: B)

Explanation: The primary goal of media literacy education is to develop critical thinking skills that enable individuals to analyze, evaluate, and understand media messages critically. It empowers students to become informed and responsible consumers and producers of media content.

Question 10:

Which of the following is an example of a summative assessment?

A) Final project

B) Pop quiz

C) Homework assignment

D) Classroom discussion

Answer: A)

Explanation: A final project is an example of a summative assessment that evaluates students' overall understanding and mastery of course content at the end of a unit or course. Summative assessments are typically used to measure student achievement and assign grades or marks.

Question 11:

In instructional design, what does the term "backwards design" refer to?

A) Starting with learning objectives and designing instruction to meet those objectives

B) Beginning with assessment tasks and designing instruction based on those tasks

C) Developing instructional materials without considering learning objectives

D) Creating assessments after instruction has already been designed

Answer: A)

Explanation: Backwards design in instructional design refers to starting with learning objectives and designing instruction to meet those objectives. It involves identifying desired learning outcomes first and then designing instructional activities, assessments, and resources to support those outcomes.

Question 12:

Which of the following is a key consideration in media literacy education?

A) Promoting uncritical acceptance of media messages

B) Encouraging passive consumption of media content

C) Developing skills for analyzing and evaluating media messages

D) Limiting access to media resources for students

Answer: C)
Explanation: A key consideration in media literacy education is developing skills for analyzing and evaluating media messages critically. Media literacy empowers students to become active and discerning consumers and producers of media content by developing critical thinking skills.

Question 13:
What is the primary purpose of a rubric in assessment?
A) To assign grades arbitrarily
B) To provide feedback to students
C) To establish clear expectations for performance
D) To limit students' creativity

Answer: C)
Explanation: The primary purpose of a rubric in assessment is to establish clear expectations for performance by outlining criteria, standards, and levels of achievement. Rubrics help students understand what is expected of them and provide a framework for evaluating their work objectively.

Question 14:
Which of the following is a characteristic of a high-quality assessment?
A) Lack of alignment with learning objectives
B) Limited opportunities for student reflection
C) Ambiguous or unclear instructions
D) Clear alignment with instructional goals and standards

Answer: D)
Explanation: A characteristic of a high-quality assessment is clear alignment with instructional goals and standards. High-quality assessments are designed to measure specific learning objectives and provide meaningful information about student performance relative to those objectives.

Question 15:
What is the purpose of formative assessment in instructional design?
A) To assign final grades to students
B) To provide ongoing feedback and support to students
C) To evaluate student learning at the end of a unit or course
D) To limit students' creativity in the learning process

Answer: B)
Explanation: The purpose of formative assessment in instructional design is to provide ongoing feedback and support to students as they progress through a unit or course. Formative assessments help educators monitor student learning and adjust instruction to meet individual student needs.

Question 16:
Which of the following is an example of an authentic assessment task?
A) True/false quiz
B) Multiple-choice test
C) Project-based assignment
D) Fill-in-the-blank worksheet

Answer: C)
Explanation: A project-based assignment is an example of an authentic assessment task that requires students to apply their knowledge and skills in a real-world context to complete a meaningful project or task.

Question 17:
What is the primary purpose of media literacy education in today's digital age?
A) To promote passive consumption of media content
B) To develop critical thinking skills for analyzing and evaluating media messages
C) To discourage students from engaging with media content
D) To limit access to media resources in educational settings

Answer: B)
Explanation: The primary purpose of media literacy education in today's digital age is to develop critical thinking skills that enable individuals to analyze, evaluate, and understand media messages critically. Media literacy empowers students to navigate the complexities of the media landscape and make informed judgments about media content.

Question 18:
Which of the following is a key consideration in media literacy education?
A) Encouraging passive consumption of media content
B) Promoting uncritical acceptance of media messages
C) Developing skills for analyzing and evaluating media messages
D) Limiting access to media resources for students

Answer: C)
Explanation: A key consideration in media literacy education is developing skills for analyzing and evaluating media messages critically. Media literacy empowers students to become active and discerning consumers and producers of media content by developing critical thinking skills.

Question 19:
What is the primary purpose of a needs assessment in instructional design?
A) To develop instructional materials without considering learner needs
B) To identify gaps in learner knowledge and skills
C) To limit access to instructional resources for students
D) To assign final grades to students

Answer: B)
Explanation: The primary purpose of a needs assessment in instructional design is to identify gaps in learner knowledge and skills and determine the specific needs and preferences of learners. Needs assessments inform the development of instructional materials and resources that address the identified needs effectively.

Question 20:
Which of the following is an example of a performance-based assessment?
A) True/false quiz
B) Multiple-choice test
C) Oral presentation
D) Fill-in-the-blank worksheet

Answer: C)
Explanation: An oral presentation is an example of a performance-based assessment that requires students to demonstrate their knowledge, skills, and abilities by presenting information orally to an audience.

Question 21:
What is the primary purpose of a media literacy curriculum?
A) To promote passive consumption of media content
B) To develop critical thinking skills for analyzing and evaluating media messages
C) To discourage students from engaging with media content
D) To limit access to media resources in educational settings

Answer: B)
Explanation: The primary purpose of a media literacy curriculum is to develop critical thinking skills that enable individuals to analyze, evaluate, and understand media messages critically. Media literacy empowers students to navigate the complexities of the media landscape and make informed judgments about media content.

Question 22:
Which of the following is a key consideration in media literacy education?
A) Encouraging passive consumption of media content
B) Promoting uncritical acceptance of media messages
C) Developing skills for analyzing and evaluating media messages
D) Limiting access to media resources for students

Answer: C)
Explanation: A key consideration in media literacy education is developing skills for analyzing and evaluating media messages critically. Media literacy empowers students to become active and discerning consumers and producers of media content by developing critical thinking skills.

Question 23:
What is the primary purpose of assessment in instructional design?
A) To assign final grades to students
B) To provide ongoing feedback to students
C) To discourage students from participating in learning activities
D) To evaluate the effectiveness of instructional materials

Answer: B)
Explanation: The primary purpose of assessment in instructional design is to provide ongoing feedback to students that informs their learning process and helps them monitor their progress towards achieving learning objectives.

Question 24:
Which of the following is an example of a formative assessment?
A) Final exam
B) Midterm project
C) Homework assignment
D) Classroom discussion

Answer: C)
Explanation: A homework assignment is an example of a formative assessment that provides ongoing feedback and support to students as they progress through a unit or course. Formative assessments help educators monitor student learning and adjust instruction accordingly.

Question 25:
What is the primary goal of media literacy education?
A) To promote passive consumption of media content
B) To develop critical thinking skills for analyzing media messages
C) To discourage students from engaging with media content
D) To limit access to media resources in educational settings

Answer: B)
Explanation: The primary goal of media literacy education is to develop critical thinking skills that enable individuals to analyze, evaluate, and understand media messages critically. Media literacy empowers students to become informed and responsible consumers and producers of media content.

Question 26:
Which of the following is an example of a summative assessment?
A) Final project
B) Pop quiz
C) Homework assignment
D) Classroom discussion

Answer: A)
Explanation: A final project is an example of a summative assessment that evaluates students' overall understanding and mastery of course content at the end of a unit or course. Summative assessments are typically used to measure student achievement and assign grades or marks.

Question 27:
What is the primary focus of media literacy education?
A) To promote uncritical consumption of media content
B) To develop critical thinking skills for analyzing media messages
C) To encourage students to believe everything they see in the media
D) To discourage students from engaging with media content

Answer: B)
Explanation: Media literacy education aims to develop critical thinking skills that enable individuals to analyze, evaluate, and understand media messages critically.

Question 28:
Which of the following is a key consideration in instructional design in educational media?
A) Creating visually appealing content
B) Aligning content with state standards
C) Meeting the diverse needs of learners
D) Incorporating the latest technology trends

Answer: C)
Explanation: Meeting the diverse needs of learners is a key consideration in instructional design in educational media.

Question 29:
What is the primary goal of media literacy education?
A) To promote passive consumption of media content
B) To develop critical thinking skills for analyzing media messages
C) To discourage students from engaging with media content
D) To limit access to media resources in educational settings

Answer: B)
Explanation: The primary goal of media literacy education is to develop critical thinking skills for analyzing media messages.

Question 30:
Which of the following is an example of a performance-based assessment?
A) True/false quiz
B) Multiple-choice test
C) Oral presentation
D) Fill-in-the-blank worksheet

Answer: C)
Explanation: An oral presentation is an example of a performance-based assessment.

Question 31:

In instructional design, what does the term "backwards design" refer to?

A) Starting with learning objectives and designing instruction to meet those objectives

B) Beginning with assessment tasks and designing instruction based on those tasks

C) Developing instructional materials without considering learning objectives

D) Creating assessments after instruction has already been designed

Answer: A)

Explanation: Backwards design in instructional design refers to starting with learning objectives and designing instruction to meet those objectives.

Question 32:

Which of the following is a characteristic of a high-quality assessment?

A) Lack of alignment with learning objectives

B) Limited opportunities for student reflection

C) Ambiguous or unclear instructions

D) Clear alignment with instructional goals and standards

Answer: D)

Explanation: Clear alignment with instructional goals and standards is a characteristic of a high-quality assessment.

Question 33:

What is the primary purpose of formative assessment in instructional design?

A) To assign final grades to students

B) To provide ongoing feedback and support to students

C) To evaluate student learning at the end of a unit or course

D) To limit students' creativity in the learning process

Answer: B)

Explanation: The primary purpose of formative assessment is to provide ongoing feedback and support to students.

Question 34:

What is the purpose of scaffolding in instructional design?

A) To make content more challenging for advanced learners

B) To provide support and guidance to learners as they develop new skills

C) To remove all support and allow learners to work independently

D) To limit access to resources for struggling learners

Answer: B)
Explanation: The purpose of scaffolding is to provide support and guidance to learners as they develop new skills.

Question 35:
Which of the following is an example of an authentic assessment?
A) Multiple-choice test
B) Essay exam
C) Portfolio review
D) True/false quiz

Answer: C)
Explanation: A portfolio review is an example of an authentic assessment.

Question 36:
What is the primary purpose of copyright law in relation to educational media?
A) To restrict access to educational materials
B) To protect the rights of creators and authors
C) To prevent educators from using media content in the classroom
D) To limit the use of digital technologies in education

Answer: B)
Explanation: The primary purpose of copyright law is to protect the rights of creators and authors.

Question 37:
Which of the following is a key consideration in media literacy education?
A) Encouraging passive consumption of media content
B) Promoting uncritical acceptance of media messages
C) Developing skills for analyzing and evaluating media messages
D) Limiting access to media resources for students

Answer: C)
Explanation: Developing skills for analyzing and evaluating media messages is a key consideration in media literacy education.

Question 38:
What is the primary purpose of a rubric in assessment?
A) To assign grades arbitrarily
B) To provide feedback to students
C) To establish clear expectations for performance
D) To limit students' creativity

Answer: C)
Explanation: The primary purpose of a rubric is to establish clear expectations for performance.

Question 39:
Which of the following is a key consideration in collection development and management for educational media specialists?
A) Acquiring materials solely based on personal preferences
B) Ignoring copyright laws and fair use guidelines
C) Balancing diverse perspectives and viewpoints
D) Limiting access to resources for students

Answer: C)
Explanation: Balancing diverse perspectives and viewpoints is a key consideration in collection development and management.

Question 40:
What is the primary purpose of a media literacy curriculum?
A) To promote passive consumption of media content
B) To develop critical thinking skills for analyzing and evaluating media messages
C) To discourage students from engaging with media content
D) To limit access to media resources in educational settings

Answer: B)
Explanation: The primary purpose of a media literacy curriculum is to develop critical thinking skills for analyzing and evaluating media messages.

Question 41:
Which of the following is an example of a summative assessment?
A) Final project
B) Pop quiz
C) Homework assignment

D) Classroom discussion

Answer: A)
Explanation: A final project is an example of a summative assessment.

Question 42:
What is the primary purpose of a needs assessment in instructional design?
A) To develop instructional materials without considering learner needs
B) To identify gaps in learner knowledge and skills
C) To limit access to instructional resources for students
D) To assign final grades to students

Answer: B)
Explanation: The primary purpose of a needs assessment is to identify gaps in learner knowledge and skills.

Question 43:
Which of the following is an example of a formative assessment?
A) Final exam
B) Midterm project
C) Homework assignment
D) Classroom discussion

Answer: C)
Explanation: A homework assignment is an example of a formative assessment.

Question 44:
What is the primary purpose of assessment in instructional design?
A) To assign final grades to students
B) To provide ongoing feedback to students
C) To discourage students from participating in learning activities
D) To evaluate the effectiveness of instructional materials

Answer: B)
Explanation: The primary purpose of assessment is to provide ongoing feedback to students.

Question 45:
Which of the following is a key consideration in media literacy education?
A) Encouraging passive consumption of media content
B) Promoting uncritical acceptance of media messages
C) Developing skills for analyzing and evaluating media messages
D) Limiting access to media resources for students

Answer: C)
Explanation: Developing skills for analyzing and evaluating media messages is a key consideration in media literacy education.

Question 46:
What is the primary focus of instructional design in educational media?
A) Creating visually appealing content
B) Aligning content with state standards
C) Meeting the diverse needs of learners
D) Incorporating the latest technology trends

Answer: C)
Explanation: Meeting the diverse needs of learners is the primary focus of instructional design in educational media.

Question 47:
Which of the following is a characteristic of a high-quality assessment?
A) Lack of alignment with learning objectives
B) Limited opportunities for student reflection
C) Ambiguous or unclear instructions
D) Clear alignment with instructional goals and standards

Answer: D)
Explanation: Clear alignment with instructional goals and standards is a characteristic of a high-quality assessment.

Question 48:
What is the primary purpose of scaffolding in instructional design?
A) To make content more challenging for advanced learners
B) To provide support and guidance to learners as they develop new skills
C) To remove all support and allow learners to work independently
D) To limit access to resources for struggling learners

Answer: B)
Explanation: The primary purpose of scaffolding is to provide support and guidance to learners as they develop new skills.

Question 49:
Which of the following is a key consideration in collection development and management for educational media specialists?
A) Acquiring materials solely based on personal preferences
B) Ignoring copyright laws and fair use guidelines
C) Balancing diverse perspectives and viewpoints
D) Limiting access to resources for students

Answer: C)
Explanation: Balancing diverse perspectives and viewpoints is a key consideration in collection development and management.

Question 50:
What is the primary purpose of a rubric in assessment?
A) To assign grades arbitrarily
B) To provide feedback to students
C) To establish clear expectations for performance
D) To limit students' creativity

Answer: C)
Explanation: The primary purpose of a rubric is to establish clear expectations for performance.

Question 51:
Which of the following is a key consideration in media literacy education?
A) Encouraging passive consumption of media content
B) Promoting uncritical acceptance of media messages
C) Developing skills for analyzing and evaluating media messages
D) Limiting access to media resources for students

Answer: C)
Explanation: Developing skills for analyzing and evaluating media messages is a key consideration in media literacy education.

Question 52:
What is the primary purpose of a media literacy curriculum?
A) To promote passive consumption of media content
B) To develop critical thinking skills for analyzing and evaluating media messages
C) To discourage students from engaging with media content
D) To limit access to media resources in educational settings

Answer: B)
Explanation: The primary purpose of a media literacy curriculum is to develop critical thinking skills for analyzing and evaluating media messages.

Question 53:
Which of the following is a characteristic of a high-quality assessment?
A) Lack of alignment with learning objectives
B) Limited opportunities for student reflection
C) Ambiguous or unclear instructions
D) Clear alignment with instructional goals and standards

Answer: D)
Explanation: Clear alignment with instructional goals and standards is a characteristic of a high-quality assessment.

Question 54:
What is the primary purpose of scaffolding in instructional design?
A) To make content more challenging for advanced learners
B) To provide support and guidance to learners as they develop new skills
C) To remove all support and allow learners to work independently
D) To limit access to resources for struggling learners

Answer: B)
Explanation: The primary purpose of scaffolding is to provide support and guidance to learners as they develop new skills.

Question 55:
Which of the following is a key consideration in collection development and management for educational media specialists?
A) Acquiring materials solely based on personal preferences
B) Ignoring copyright laws and fair use guidelines
C) Balancing diverse perspectives and viewpoints

D) Limiting access to resources for students

Answer: C)
Explanation: Balancing diverse perspectives and viewpoints is a key consideration in collection development and management.

Question 56:
What is the primary purpose of a rubric in assessment?
A) To assign grades arbitrarily
B) To provide feedback to students
C) To establish clear expectations for performance
D) To limit students' creativity

Answer: C)
Explanation: The primary purpose of a rubric is to establish clear expectations for performance.

Question 57:
Which of the following is a key consideration in media literacy education?
A) Encouraging passive consumption of media content
B) Promoting uncritical acceptance of media messages
C) Developing skills for analyzing and evaluating media messages
D) Limiting access to media resources for students

Answer: C)
Explanation: Developing skills for analyzing and evaluating media messages is a key consideration in media literacy education.

Question 58:
What is the primary purpose of a media literacy curriculum?
A) To promote passive consumption of media content
B) To develop critical thinking skills for analyzing and evaluating media messages
C) To discourage students from engaging with media content
D) To limit access to media resources in educational settings

Answer: B)
Explanation: The primary purpose of a media literacy curriculum is to develop critical thinking skills for analyzing and evaluating media messages.

Question 59:

Which of the following is a characteristic of a high-quality assessment?

A) Lack of alignment with learning objectives

B) Limited opportunities for student reflection

C) Ambiguous or unclear instructions

D) Clear alignment with instructional goals and standards

Answer: D)

Explanation: Clear alignment with instructional goals and standards is a characteristic of a high-quality assessment.

Question 60:

What is the primary purpose of scaffolding in instructional design?

A) To make content more challenging for advanced learners

B) To provide support and guidance to learners as they develop new skills

C) To remove all support and allow learners to work independently

D) To limit access to resources for struggling learners

Answer: B)

Explanation: The primary purpose of scaffolding is to provide support and guidance to learners as they develop new skills.

Question 61:

Which of the following is a key consideration in collection development and management for educational media specialists?

A) Acquiring materials solely based on personal preferences

B) Ignoring copyright laws and fair use guidelines

C) Balancing diverse perspectives and viewpoints

D) Limiting access to resources for students

Answer: C)

Explanation: Balancing diverse perspectives and viewpoints is a key consideration in collection development and management.

Question 62:

What is the primary purpose of a rubric in assessment?

A) To assign grades arbitrarily

B) To provide feedback to students

C) To establish clear expectations for performance

D) To limit students' creativity

Answer: C)
Explanation: The primary purpose of a rubric is to establish clear expectations for performance.

Question 63:
Which of the following is a key consideration in media literacy education?
A) Encouraging passive consumption of media content
B) Promoting uncritical acceptance of media messages
C) Developing skills for analyzing and evaluating media messages
D) Limiting access to media resources for students

Answer: C)
Explanation: Developing skills for analyzing and evaluating media messages is a key consideration in media literacy education.

Question 64:
What is the primary purpose of a media literacy curriculum?
A) To promote passive consumption of media content
B) To develop critical thinking skills for analyzing and evaluating media messages
C) To discourage students from engaging with media content
D) To limit access to media resources in educational settings

Answer: B)
Explanation: The primary purpose of a media literacy curriculum is to develop critical thinking skills for analyzing and evaluating media messages.

Question 65:
Which of the following is a characteristic of a high-quality assessment?
A) Lack of alignment with learning objectives
B) Limited opportunities for student reflection
C) Ambiguous or unclear instructions
D) Clear alignment with instructional goals and standards

Answer: D)
Explanation: Clear alignment with instructional goals and standards is a characteristic of a high-quality assessment.

Question 66:
What is the primary purpose of scaffolding in instructional design?
A) To make content more challenging for advanced learners
B) To provide support and guidance to learners as they develop new skills
C) To remove all support and allow learners to work independently
D) To limit access to resources for struggling learners

Answer: B)
Explanation: The primary purpose of scaffolding is to provide support and guidance to learners as they develop new skills.

Question 67:
Which of the following is a key consideration in collection development and management for educational media specialists?
A) Acquiring materials solely based on personal preferences
B) Ignoring copyright laws and fair use guidelines
C) Balancing diverse perspectives and viewpoints
D) Limiting access to resources for students

Answer: C)
Explanation: Balancing diverse perspectives and viewpoints is a key consideration in collection development and management.

Question 68:
What is the primary purpose of a rubric in assessment?
A) To assign grades arbitrarily
B) To provide feedback to students
C) To establish clear expectations for performance
D) To limit students' creativity

Answer: C)
Explanation: The primary purpose of a rubric is to establish clear expectations for performance.

Question 69:
Which of the following is a key consideration in media literacy education?
A) Encouraging passive consumption of media content
B) Promoting uncritical acceptance of media messages
C) Developing skills for analyzing and evaluating media messages
D) Limiting access to media resources for students

Answer: C)
Explanation: Developing skills for analyzing and evaluating media messages is a key consideration in media literacy education.

Question 70:
What is the primary purpose of a media literacy curriculum?
A) To promote passive consumption of media content
B) To develop critical thinking skills for analyzing and evaluating media messages
C) To discourage students from engaging with media content
D) To limit access to media resources in educational settings

Answer: B)
Explanation: The primary purpose of a media literacy curriculum is to develop critical thinking skills for analyzing and evaluating media messages.

Question 71:
What is the primary focus of media literacy education?
A) To promote uncritical consumption of media content
B) To develop critical thinking skills for analyzing media messages
C) To encourage students to believe everything they see in the media
D) To discourage students from engaging with media content

Answer: B)
Explanation: Media literacy education focuses on developing critical thinking skills for analyzing media messages.

Question 72:
Which of the following is a key consideration in instructional design in educational media?
A) Creating visually appealing content
B) Aligning content with state standards
C) Meeting the diverse needs of learners
D) Incorporating the latest technology trends

Answer: C)
Explanation: Meeting the diverse needs of learners is a key consideration in instructional design in educational media.

Question 73:
What is the primary goal of media literacy education?
A) To promote passive consumption of media content
B) To develop critical thinking skills for analyzing media messages
C) To discourage students from engaging with media content
D) To limit access to media resources in educational settings

Answer: B)
Explanation: The primary goal of media literacy education is to develop critical thinking skills for analyzing media messages.

Question 74:
Which of the following is an example of a performance-based assessment?
A) True/false quiz
B) Multiple-choice test
C) Oral presentation
D) Fill-in-the-blank worksheet

Answer: C)
Explanation: An oral presentation is a performance-based assessment.

Question 75:
In instructional design, what does the term "backwards design" refer to?
A) Starting with learning objectives and designing instruction to meet those objectives
B) Beginning with assessment tasks and designing instruction based on those tasks
C) Developing instructional materials without considering learning objectives
D) Creating assessments after instruction has already been designed

Answer: A)
Explanation: Backwards design involves starting with learning objectives and designing instruction to meet those objectives.

Question 76:
Which of the following is a characteristic of a high-quality assessment?
A) Lack of alignment with learning objectives
B) Limited opportunities for student reflection
C) Ambiguous or unclear instructions
D) Clear alignment with instructional goals and standards

Answer: D)
Explanation: Clear alignment with instructional goals and standards is a characteristic of a high-quality assessment.

Question 77:
What is the primary purpose of formative assessment in instructional design?
A) To assign final grades to students
B) To provide ongoing feedback and support to students
C) To evaluate student learning at the end of a unit or course
D) To limit students' creativity in the learning process

Answer: B)
Explanation: The primary purpose of formative assessment is to provide ongoing feedback and support to students.

Question 78:
What is the purpose of scaffolding in instructional design?
A) To make content more challenging for advanced learners
B) To provide support and guidance to learners as they develop new skills
C) To remove all support and allow learners to work independently
D) To limit access to resources for struggling learners

Answer: B)
Explanation: Scaffolding provides support and guidance to learners as they develop new skills.

Question 79:
Which of the following is an example of an authentic assessment?
A) Multiple-choice test
B) Essay exam
C) Portfolio review
D) True/false quiz

Answer: C)
Explanation: A portfolio review is an example of an authentic assessment.

Question 80:
What is the primary purpose of copyright law in relation to educational media?
A) To restrict access to educational materials
B) To protect the rights of creators and authors
C) To prevent educators from using media content in the classroom
D) To limit the use of digital technologies in education

Answer: B)
Explanation: Copyright law protects the rights of creators and authors.

Question 81:
Which of the following is a key consideration in media literacy education?
A) Encouraging passive consumption of media content
B) Promoting uncritical acceptance of media messages
C) Developing skills for analyzing and evaluating media messages
D) Limiting access to media resources for students

Answer: C)
Explanation: Media literacy education focuses on developing skills for analyzing and evaluating media messages.

Question 82:
What is the primary purpose of a rubric in assessment?
A) To assign grades arbitrarily
B) To provide feedback to students
C) To establish clear expectations for performance
D) To limit students' creativity

Answer: C)
Explanation: A rubric establishes clear expectations for performance.

Question 83:
Which of the following is a key consideration in collection development and management for educational media specialists?
A) Acquiring materials solely based on personal preferences
B) Ignoring copyright laws and fair use guidelines
C) Balancing diverse perspectives and viewpoints
D) Limiting access to resources for students

Answer: C)
Explanation: Collection development should balance diverse perspectives and viewpoints.

Question 84:
What is the primary purpose of a media literacy curriculum?
A) To promote passive consumption of media content
B) To develop critical thinking skills for analyzing and evaluating media messages
C) To discourage students from engaging with media content
D) To limit access to media resources in educational settings

Answer: B)
Explanation: The primary purpose of a media literacy curriculum is to develop critical thinking skills.

Question 85:
Which of the following is a characteristic of a high-quality assessment?
A) Lack of alignment with learning objectives
B) Limited opportunities for student reflection
C) Ambiguous or unclear instructions
D) Clear alignment with instructional goals and standards

Answer: D)
Explanation: High-quality assessments align with instructional goals and standards.

Question 86:
What is the primary purpose of scaffolding in instructional design?
A) To make content more challenging for advanced learners
B) To provide support and guidance to learners as they develop new skills
C) To remove all support and allow learners to work independently
D) To limit access to resources for struggling learners

Answer: B)
Explanation: Scaffolding provides support and guidance to learners.

Question 87:
Which of the following is a key consideration in collection development and management for educational media specialists?
A) Acquiring materials solely based on personal preferences
B) Ignoring copyright laws and fair use guidelines
C) Balancing diverse perspectives and viewpoints
D) Limiting access to resources for students

Answer: C)
Explanation: Collection development should balance diverse perspectives.

Question 88:
What is the primary purpose of a rubric in assessment?
A) To assign grades arbitrarily
B) To provide feedback to students
C) To establish clear expectations for performance
D) To limit students' creativity

Answer: C)
Explanation: A rubric establishes clear expectations for performance.

Question 89:
Which of the following is a key consideration in media literacy education?
A) Encouraging passive consumption of media content
B) Promoting uncritical acceptance of media messages
C) Developing skills for analyzing and evaluating media messages
D) Limiting access to media resources for students

Answer: C)
Explanation: Media literacy education focuses on developing skills for analyzing and evaluating media messages.

Question 90:
What is the primary purpose of a media literacy curriculum?
A) To promote passive consumption of media content
B) To develop critical thinking skills for analyzing and evaluating media messages
C) To discourage students from engaging with media content
D) To limit access to media resources in educational settings

Answer: B)
Explanation: The primary purpose of a media literacy curriculum is to develop critical thinking skills.

Question 91:

Which of the following is a characteristic of a high-quality assessment?
A) Lack of alignment with learning objectives
B) Limited opportunities for student reflection
C) Ambiguous or unclear instructions
D) Clear alignment with instructional goals and standards

Answer: D)
Explanation: High-quality assessments align with instructional goals and standards.

Question 92:

What is the primary purpose of scaffolding in instructional design?
A) To make content more challenging for advanced learners
B) To provide support and guidance to learners as they develop new skills
C) To remove all support and allow learners to work independently
D) To limit access to resources for struggling learners

Answer: B)
Explanation: Scaffolding provides support and guidance to learners.

Question 93:

Which of the following is a key consideration in collection development and management for educational media specialists?
A) Acquiring materials solely based on personal preferences
B) Ignoring copyright laws and fair use guidelines
C) Balancing diverse perspectives and viewpoints
D) Limiting access to resources for students

Answer: C)
Explanation: Collection development should balance diverse perspectives.

Question 94:

What is the primary purpose of a rubric in assessment?
A) To assign grades arbitrarily
B) To provide feedback to students

C) To establish clear expectations for performance
D) To limit students' creativity

Answer: C)
Explanation: A rubric establishes clear expectations for performance.

Question 95:
Which of the following is a key consideration in media literacy education?
A) Encouraging passive consumption of media content
B) Promoting uncritical acceptance of media messages
C) Developing skills for analyzing and evaluating media messages
D) Limiting access to media resources for students

Answer: C)
Explanation: Media literacy education focuses on developing skills for analyzing and evaluating media messages.

Question 96:
What is the primary purpose of a media literacy curriculum?
A) To promote passive consumption of media content
B) To develop critical thinking skills for analyzing and evaluating media messages
C) To discourage students from engaging with media content
D) To limit access to media resources in educational settings

Answer: B)
Explanation: The primary purpose of a media literacy curriculum is to develop critical thinking skills.

Question 97:
Which of the following is a characteristic of a high-quality assessment?
A) Lack of alignment with learning objectives
B) Limited opportunities for student reflection
C) Ambiguous or unclear instructions
D) Clear alignment with instructional goals and standards

Answer: D)
Explanation: High-quality assessments align with instructional goals and standards.

Question 98:
What is the primary purpose of scaffolding in instructional design?
A) To make content more challenging for advanced learners
B) To provide support and guidance to learners as they develop new skills
C) To remove all support and allow learners to work independently
D) To limit access to resources for struggling learners

Answer: B)
Explanation: Scaffolding provides support and guidance to learners.

Question 99:
Which of the following is a key consideration in collection development and management for educational media specialists?
A) Acquiring materials solely based on personal preferences
B) Ignoring copyright laws and fair use guidelines
C) Balancing diverse perspectives and viewpoints
D) Limiting access to resources for students

Answer: C)
Explanation: Collection development should balance diverse perspectives.

Question 100:
What is the primary purpose of a rubric in assessment?
A) To assign grades arbitrarily
B) To provide feedback to students
C) To establish clear expectations for performance
D) To limit students' creativity

Answer: C)
Explanation: A rubric establishes clear expectations for performance.

Question 101:
Which of the following best describes the primary goal of media literacy education?
A) To promote passive consumption of media content
B) To develop critical thinking skills for analyzing media messages
C) To encourage students to accept media messages without question
D) To discourage students from engaging with media content

Answer: B)

Explanation: The primary goal of media literacy education is to develop critical thinking skills for analyzing media messages.

Question 102:

In instructional design, what is the significance of backward design?

A) It involves designing assessments before developing learning objectives.

B) It starts with identifying learning objectives and then designing instruction to meet those objectives.

C) It emphasizes creating instructional materials without considering learning objectives.

D) It focuses on technology trends rather than aligning content with standards.

Answer: B)

Explanation: Backward design entails identifying learning objectives and then designing instruction to meet those objectives.

Question 103:

Which of the following is a crucial consideration in collection development for educational media specialists?

A) Prioritizing personal preferences in selecting materials

B) Disregarding copyright laws and fair use guidelines

C) Maintaining a narrow focus to cater to specific interests

D) Ensuring a balanced representation of diverse perspectives

Answer: D)

Explanation: A crucial consideration in collection development is ensuring a balanced representation of diverse perspectives.

Question 104:

What is the primary objective of scaffolding in instructional design?

A) To limit access to resources for struggling learners

B) To make content more challenging for advanced learners

C) To remove all support and encourage independent work

D) To provide support and guidance to learners as they develop new skills

Answer: D)

Explanation: Scaffolding aims to provide support and guidance to learners as they develop new skills.

Question 105:

Which of the following is an example of a formative assessment?

A) Final exam

B) Midterm project

C) Homework assignment

D) Classroom discussion

Answer: C)

Explanation: A homework assignment is an example of formative assessment.

Question 106:

What is the primary purpose of formative assessment in instructional design?

A) To assign final grades to students

B) To provide ongoing feedback and support to students

C) To evaluate student learning at the end of a unit or course

D) To limit students' creativity in the learning process

Answer: B)

Explanation: The primary purpose of formative assessment is to provide ongoing feedback and support to students.

Question 107:

In media literacy education, what is the significance of developing critical thinking skills?

A) To encourage uncritical acceptance of media messages

B) To promote passive consumption of media content

C) To enable students to analyze and evaluate media messages effectively

D) To discourage students from engaging with media content

Answer: C)

Explanation: Developing critical thinking skills enables students to analyze and evaluate media messages effectively.

Question 108:

Which of the following is a characteristic of a high-quality assessment?

A) Lack of alignment with learning objectives

B) Limited opportunities for student reflection

C) Ambiguous or unclear instructions

D) Clear alignment with instructional goals and standards

Answer: D)
Explanation: Clear alignment with instructional goals and standards is a characteristic of high-quality assessments.

Question 109:
What is the primary purpose of media literacy education?
A) To promote passive consumption of media content
B) To develop critical thinking skills for analyzing media messages
C) To discourage students from engaging with media content
D) To limit access to media resources in educational settings

Answer: B)
Explanation: The primary purpose of media literacy education is to develop critical thinking skills for analyzing media messages.

Question 110:
Which of the following is a key consideration in instructional design in educational media?
A) Creating visually appealing content
B) Aligning content with state standards
C) Meeting the diverse needs of learners
D) Incorporating the latest technology trends

Answer: C)
Explanation: Meeting the diverse needs of learners is a key consideration in instructional design in educational media.

Question 111:
What is the primary goal of media literacy education?
A) To promote passive consumption of media content
B) To develop critical thinking skills for analyzing media messages
C) To discourage students from engaging with media content
D) To limit access to media resources in educational settings

Answer: B)
Explanation: The primary goal of media literacy education is to develop critical thinking skills for analyzing media messages.

Question 112:
Which of the following is an example of a performance-based assessment?
A) True/false quiz
B) Multiple-choice test
C) Oral presentation
D) Fill-in-the-blank worksheet

Answer: C)
Explanation: An oral presentation is a performance-based assessment.

Question 113:
In instructional design, what does the term "backwards design" refer to?
A) Starting with learning objectives and designing instruction to meet those objectives
B) Beginning with assessment tasks and designing instruction based on those tasks
C) Developing instructional materials without considering learning objectives
D) Creating assessments after instruction has already been designed

Answer: A)
Explanation: Backwards design involves starting with learning objectives and designing instruction to meet those objectives.

Question 114:
Which of the following is a characteristic of a high-quality assessment?
A) Lack of alignment with learning objectives
B) Limited opportunities for student reflection
C) Ambiguous or unclear instructions
D) Clear alignment with instructional goals and standards

Answer: D)
Explanation: Clear alignment with instructional goals and standards is a characteristic of high-quality assessments.

Question 115:
What is the primary purpose of formative assessment in instructional design?
A) To assign final grades to students
B) To provide ongoing feedback and support to students
C) To evaluate student learning at the end of a unit or course
D) To limit students' creativity in the learning process

Answer: B)
Explanation: The primary purpose of formative assessment is to provide ongoing feedback and support to students.

Question 116:
What is the purpose of scaffolding in instructional design?
A) To make content more challenging for advanced learners
B) To provide support and guidance to learners as they develop new skills
C) To remove all support and allow learners to work independently
D) To limit access to resources for struggling learners

Answer: B)
Explanation: Scaffolding provides support and guidance to learners as they develop new skills.

Question 117:
Which of the following is an example of an authentic assessment?
A) Multiple-choice test
B) Essay exam
C) Portfolio review
D) True/false quiz

Answer: C)
Explanation: A portfolio review is an example of an authentic assessment.

Question 118:
What is the primary purpose of copyright law in relation to educational media?
A) To restrict access to educational materials
B) To protect the rights of creators and authors
C) To prevent educators from using media content in the classroom
D) To limit the use of digital technologies in education

Answer: B)
Explanation: Copyright law protects the rights of creators and authors.

Question 119:
Which of the following is a key consideration in media literacy education?
A) Encouraging passive consumption of media content
B) Promoting uncritical acceptance of media messages
C) Developing skills for analyzing and evaluating media messages
D) Limiting access to media resources for students

Answer: C)
Explanation: Media literacy education focuses on developing skills for analyzing and evaluating media messages.

Question 120:
What is the primary purpose of a rubric in assessment?
A) To assign grades arbitrarily
B) To provide feedback to students
C) To establish clear expectations for performance
D) To limit students' creativity

Answer: C)
Explanation: A rubric establishes clear expectations for performance.

Question 121:
Which of the following is a key consideration in collection development and management for educational media specialists?
A) Acquiring materials solely based on personal preferences
B) Ignoring copyright laws and fair use guidelines
C) Balancing diverse perspectives and viewpoints
D) Limiting access to resources for students

Answer: C)
Explanation: Collection development should balance diverse perspectives and viewpoints.

Question 122:
What is the primary purpose of a media literacy curriculum?
A) To promote passive consumption of media content
B) To develop critical thinking skills for analyzing and evaluating media messages
C) To discourage students from engaging with media content
D) To limit access to media resources in educational settings

Answer: B)
Explanation: The primary purpose of a media literacy curriculum is to develop critical thinking skills.

Question 123:
Which of the following is a characteristic of a high-quality assessment?
A) Lack of alignment with learning objectives
B) Limited opportunities for student reflection
C) Ambiguous or unclear instructions
D) Clear alignment with instructional goals and standards

Answer: D)
Explanation: High-quality assessments align with instructional goals and standards.

Question 124:
What is the primary purpose of scaffolding in instructional design?
A) To make content more challenging for advanced learners
B) To provide support and guidance to learners as they develop new skills
C) To remove all support and allow learners to work independently
D) To limit access to resources for struggling learners

Answer: B)
Explanation: Scaffolding provides support and guidance to learners.

Question 125:
Which of the following is a key consideration in collection development and management for educational media specialists?
A) Acquiring materials solely based on personal preferences
B) Ignoring copyright laws and fair use guidelines
C) Balancing diverse perspectives and viewpoints
D) Limiting access to resources for students

Answer: C)
Explanation: Collection development should balance diverse perspectives.

Question 126:
What is the primary purpose of a rubric in assessment?
A) To assign grades arbitrarily
B) To provide feedback to students
C) To establish clear expectations for performance
D) To limit students' creativity

Answer: C)
Explanation: A rubric establishes clear expectations for performance.

Question 127:
Which of the following is a key consideration in media literacy education?
A) Encouraging passive consumption of media content
B) Promoting uncritical acceptance of media messages
C) Developing skills for analyzing and evaluating media messages
D) Limiting access to media resources for students

Answer: C)
Explanation: Media literacy education focuses on developing skills for analyzing and evaluating media messages.

Question 128:
What is the primary purpose of a media literacy curriculum?
A) To promote passive consumption of media content
B) To develop critical thinking skills for analyzing and evaluating media messages
C) To discourage students from engaging with media content
D) To limit access to media resources in educational settings

Answer: B)
Explanation: The primary purpose of a media literacy curriculum is to develop critical thinking skills.

Question 129:
Which of the following is a characteristic of a high-quality assessment?
A) Lack of alignment with learning objectives
B) Limited opportunities for student reflection
C) Ambiguous or unclear instructions
D) Clear alignment with instructional goals and standards

Answer: D)

Explanation: High-quality assessments align with instructional goals and standards.

Question 130:

What is the primary purpose of scaffolding in instructional design?

A) To make content more challenging for advanced learners

B) To provide support and guidance to learners as they develop new skills

C) To remove all support and allow learners to work independently

D) To limit access to resources for struggling learners

Answer: B)

Explanation: Scaffolding provides support and guidance to learners.

Question 131:

What is the primary focus of media literacy education?

A) To promote passive consumption of media content

B) To develop critical thinking skills for analyzing media messages

C) To encourage students to believe everything they see in the media

D) To discourage students from engaging with media content

Answer: B)

Explanation: The primary focus of media literacy education is to develop critical thinking skills for analyzing media messages.

Question 132:

Which of the following is a key consideration in instructional design in educational media?

A) Creating visually appealing content

B) Aligning content with state standards

C) Meeting the diverse needs of learners

D) Incorporating the latest technology trends

Answer: C)

Explanation: Meeting the diverse needs of learners is a key consideration in instructional design in educational media.

Question 133:

What is the primary goal of media literacy education?

A) To promote passive consumption of media content

B) To develop critical thinking skills for analyzing media messages

C) To discourage students from engaging with media content

D) To limit access to media resources in educational settings

Answer: B)

Explanation: The primary goal of media literacy education is to develop critical thinking skills for analyzing media messages.

Question 134:

Which of the following is a key consideration in collection development for educational media specialists?

A) Prioritizing personal preferences in selecting materials

B) Disregarding copyright laws and fair use guidelines

C) Maintaining a narrow focus to cater to specific interests

D) Ensuring a balanced representation of diverse perspectives

Answer: D)

Explanation: A key consideration in collection development is ensuring a balanced representation of diverse perspectives.

Question 135:

What is the primary objective of scaffolding in instructional design?

A) To limit access to resources for struggling learners

B) To make content more challenging for advanced learners

C) To remove all support and encourage independent work

D) To provide support and guidance to learners as they develop new skills

Answer: D)

Explanation: The primary objective of scaffolding is to provide support and guidance to learners as they develop new skills.

Question 136:

Which of the following is an example of a formative assessment?

A) Final exam

B) Midterm project

C) Homework assignment

D) Classroom discussion

Answer: C)
Explanation: A homework assignment is an example of a formative assessment.

Question 137:
What is the primary purpose of formative assessment in instructional design?
A) To assign final grades to students
B) To provide ongoing feedback and support to students
C) To evaluate student learning at the end of a unit or course
D) To limit students' creativity in the learning process

Answer: B)
Explanation: The primary purpose of formative assessment is to provide ongoing feedback and support to students.

Question 138:
In media literacy education, what is the significance of developing critical thinking skills?
A) To encourage uncritical acceptance of media messages
B) To promote passive consumption of media content
C) To enable students to analyze and evaluate media messages effectively
D) To discourage students from engaging with media content

Answer: C)
Explanation: Developing critical thinking skills enables students to analyze and evaluate media messages effectively.

Question 139:
Which of the following is a characteristic of a high-quality assessment?
A) Lack of alignment with learning objectives
B) Limited opportunities for student reflection
C) Ambiguous or unclear instructions
D) Clear alignment with instructional goals and standards

Answer: D)
Explanation: Clear alignment with instructional goals and standards is a characteristic of high-quality assessments.

Question 140:
What is the primary purpose of media literacy education?
A) To promote passive consumption of media content
B) To develop critical thinking skills for analyzing media messages
C) To discourage students from engaging with media content
D) To limit access to media resources in educational settings

Answer: B)
Explanation: The primary purpose of media literacy education is to develop critical thinking skills for analyzing media messages.

Question 141:
Which of the following is an example of a performance-based assessment?
A) True/false quiz
B) Multiple-choice test
C) Oral presentation
D) Fill-in-the-blank worksheet

Answer: C)
Explanation: An oral presentation is a performance-based assessment.

Question 142:
In instructional design, what does the term "backwards design" refer to?
A) Starting with learning objectives and designing instruction to meet those objectives
B) Beginning with assessment tasks and designing instruction based on those tasks
C) Developing instructional materials without considering learning objectives
D) Creating assessments after instruction has already been designed

Answer: A)
Explanation: Backwards design involves starting with learning objectives and designing instruction to meet those objectives.

Question 143:
Which of the following is a characteristic of a high-quality assessment?
A) Lack of alignment with learning objectives
B) Limited opportunities for student reflection
C) Ambiguous or unclear instructions
D) Clear alignment with instructional goals and standards

Answer: D)
Explanation: Clear alignment with instructional goals and standards is a characteristic of high-quality assessments.

Question 144:
What is the primary purpose of formative assessment in instructional design?
A) To assign final grades to students
B) To provide ongoing feedback and support to students
C) To evaluate student learning at the end of a unit or course
D) To limit students' creativity in the learning process

Answer: B)
Explanation: The primary purpose of formative assessment is to provide ongoing feedback and support to students.

Question 145:
What is the purpose of scaffolding in instructional design?
A) To make content more challenging for advanced learners
B) To provide support and guidance to learners as they develop new skills
C) To remove all support and allow learners to work independently
D) To limit access to resources for struggling learners

Answer: B)
Explanation: Scaffolding provides support and guidance to learners as they develop new skills.

Question 146:
Which of the following is an example of an authentic assessment?
A) Multiple-choice test
B) Essay exam
C) Portfolio review
D) True/false quiz

Answer: C)
Explanation: A portfolio review is an example of an authentic assessment.

Question 147:
What is the primary purpose of copyright law in relation to educational media?
A) To restrict access to educational materials
B) To protect the rights of creators and authors
C) To prevent educators from using media content in the classroom
D) To limit the use of digital technologies in education

Answer: B)
Explanation: Copyright law protects the rights of creators and authors.

Question 148:
Which of the following is a key consideration in media literacy education?
A) Encouraging passive consumption of media content
B) Promoting uncritical acceptance of media messages
C) Developing skills for analyzing and evaluating media messages
D) Limiting access to media resources for students

Answer: C)
Explanation: Media literacy education focuses on developing skills for analyzing and evaluating media messages.

Question 149:
What is the primary purpose of a rubric in assessment?
A) To assign grades arbitrarily
B) To provide feedback to students
C) To establish clear expectations for performance
D) To limit students' creativity

Answer: C)
Explanation: A rubric establishes clear expectations for performance.

Question 150:
Which of the following is a key consideration in collection development and management for educational media specialists?
A) Acquiring materials solely based on personal preferences
B) Ignoring copyright laws and fair use guidelines
C) Balancing diverse perspectives and viewpoints
D) Limiting access to resources for students

Answer: C)
Explanation: Collection development should balance diverse perspectives.

Made in United States
Orlando, FL
11 December 2024

55453933R00050